God Knows Where I Am

Volume One

The Wilderness Experience

NAVAJO COUNTRY

NAVAJO COUNTRY

THE DIRT ROAD UP HILL TO WHEATFIELDS

God Knows Where I Am
Volume One

The Wilderness Experience

By Lynn Cartwright

Copyright © 2006 by Lynn Cartwright
Original copyright © 2000 by Lynn Cartwright

God Knows Where I Am
by Lynn Cartwright

Printed in the United States of America

ISBN 1-60034-296-5

All rights reserved solely by the author. The author guarantees all contents are original and do not infringe upon the legal rights of any other person or work. No part of this book may be reproduced in any form without the permission of the author. The views expressed in this book are not necessarily those of the publisher.

Unless otherwise indicated, Bible quotations are taken from the King James Version of the Bible.

www.xulonpress.com

Contents

Foreword ix
Acknowledgements xi

Chapters

1. Real People 13
2. Chee 17
3. The Way Home 23
4. A Pile of Suns 33
5. What Is Thanksgiving? 41
6. Tell Me the Story of Jesus 53
7. Watch What You Discard 61
8. For Each Other 69
9. A Narrow Road Rising Up 77
10. Big Texas Style Toast 85
11. Under the Shadow of the Almighty 91
12. Do We Have to Do It This Way? 95
13. Did I Really Pray That? 101
14. In His Hands—THE ROYAL SUITE 105

Epilogue 109
Many Waters Mission Today 113

Blue bus at Sanostee, NM on way to Wheatfields, AZ

Foreword

High in the remote mountains of northeastern Arizona, a Navajo family was asking God to send someone to teach them.

Meanwhile, in Columbus, Ohio, a family of six was praying to find God's perfect will for their lives. They did not know about the Navajo family's prayer, and would never have dreamed of uprooting their family and moving to a mountaintop with no real house, no running water, no electricity, no kitchen, no job, no place to even get a job, and few people who spoke English. However, leaving behind all that was familiar except each other and their faith, they packed a few basic supplies into a used, powder blue school bus, and traveled west.

This is the story of love and learning that went in both directions as they lived that first year on the mountain among the Navajo People.

Karen S. Yost
April 2006

Acknowledgements

For years, I hoped to publish the story of our experiences and God's blessings, but finding time to write was hard. With the encouragement of Margot Bass and Dorothy Bass, I began to write *The Wilderness Experience* while they continued to encourage me and edit my manuscript.

Years later, David and Karen Keller determined to publish the book and began the serious job of finding a publisher and completing the editing of the manuscript. Their friend, Salene Schaffer, encouraged, educated, and helped them with the preparation. I am very grateful for their hard work.

May God bless all of them for their dedication to Him and their love to us here at the Many Waters Mission.

Chapter 1

Real People

Night coming down! Wrapped in its black velvet clutches, I eased my way around the stones that kept our fire from spreading too far, and lit the pine needles. The tiny glow, melting the darkness away, began to lift the gloom of the evening. Howling coyotes added a mysterious symphonic tone to the pounding of peyote drums not far down the mountain. Someone—or something—walked stealthily past me not more than ten feet away—just awareness of a presence—then nothing.

The leaping flames now created ghostly shadows in the tall white pines. I wondered who, or what, was out there. Questioning the wisdom of moving at all, I reached for firewood and was startled by the clanking of metal—the coffee pot! What a comforting idea. Black and grungy from being deposited in the middle of so many fires, the pot's leftover coffee sounded good. I began to be conscious of every move I made, with an eerie feeling that comes from sensing something wrong, but no concrete evidence to base that feeling on.

Daring me even to see it, a sliver of moon came into view. As though in conspiracy, a great sinister cloud covered it before its light illumined any of my mountaintop, and the coyotes complained bitterly.

What a strange place for me, a lover of creature comforts, to be—high in the Arizona mountains on the Navajo Indian Reservation, with only a big blue school bus to call home. Huddling close to the fire, I looked behind me at the bus. Our four-year-old daughter was sleeping inside, the door closed securely.

Muffled cursing and the sound of breaking glass shattered my thoughts. The sound was at least a hundred yards away.

"Lynn?"

Right under my elbow, eight pairs of deep brown eyes looked at me, and a ten-year-old voice said, "Will you watch these children? Their families are drunk and fighting, and the other little ones got scared and ran away. We have to find them quickly." And then softly, she was gone, leaving me with seven teary-eyed little ones who were almost as afraid of this white woman as they were of the fighting and the darkness.

The big sinister cloud was cobwebbing its way across the sky now, torn apart by winds that were fighting with my fire. I traded the coffee for hot Navajo tea and began to put down blankets—one to sit on and one to cuddle in.

"What's going on?"

"Oh, Don, thank God you're here! Everybody down at the first house is drunk, and they're all fighting. Will you go down there and see if you can do something?" I don't know what I expected my husband to do.

In less than ten minutes, he was back. "It's over. Everybody else was hiding in the pines. Chester lassoed one of the boys and tied him to a tree. Most of them will sleep it off now."

It seemed hours before someone came for the children. The maddened drunks slipped into the stupor that signaled peace for the babies and the worried great grandfather.

Swollen eyes, broken teeth, and churning stomachs would reign tomorrow. At least all the little ones had been accounted for. Three generations of people who cared about each other—all drunk and trying to hurt those closest to them.

I listened to the peyote drums far into the night and wet my pillow with many tears as I prayed, *God, give us a way to put an end to this. Not a dime in our pockets; hardly anyone even knows that we're here. These aren't just names. These are real people who touch me and mingle their tears with mine. There must be answers for them.*

The questions continued to come as I tossed and turned and wondered about the days ahead. There was nothing concrete in our future. How had we come to be here on this mountaintop—my husband, our four children and I? We were doing our laundry in a mountain stream, cooking all our meals over a campfire, and praying every day for the next meal to come—trying to survive the rugged country with no income and nothing but beds, a few clothes, and cooking utensils—and feeling overwhelmed at times by the physical and spiritual needs all around us. Wasn't it just yesterday that my husband was looking forward to his vacation paycheck, a short mission trip to the Navajo Reservation, and then a return to our four-bedroom home and to his job?

Two years in a row we had brought our missionary team across the country from Ohio to Oklahoma, Arizona, and New Mexico. The first tour had been filled with unexplainable events—that is, unexplainable without God—that startled us into realizing that God really was intimately involved with the daily happenings of our lives. So many things—the van we were driving blew an engine, and through a series of unusual events, a stranger loaned us his to continue the trip, even though he had never seen us before and we were traveling a thousand miles from his home. Step by step, the Lord led us until the people and their need to know Jesus held our hearts captive. And then the day came when we knew we were to go to New Mexico and stay. We didn't know how; we didn't know where; but God said he would make a way.

I don't know why I wasn't terrified. The idea of leaving home and job and family for the unknown really should have frightened us. But we had tasted the knowing—knowing God as Lord of everything. We had watched him supply food when it was needed, beds when they were needed, gasoline when it was needed, and most of all, answer the questions of hurting people, letting them know there really is a God, and he really does care!

CHAPTER 2

Chee

It was still summer, and the wonderful smell of the cooking fires woke us early. Our Navajo friends told us that when morning comes, God looks around to see who is up and who is still sleeping. They believe that God will not help you through that day if you are not up early.

I wondered how that idea would apply to people who work night shift in hospitals and other places, and I began to think again how wonderful God is, who never sleeps and never slumbers and who knows what is best for his children.

This morning we had some important survival needs. The water barrel had less than two quarts of water in it, and the spring was a mile and a half away. No problem if you have a vehicle, but our only transportation, the blue school bus, had a blown engine. The only answer was to get buckets and walk—a mile and a half with empty buckets for Don and our sons, Brian, Brett, and Brad, and then a mile and a half back with full ones. I was thankful for those strong muscles carrying those buckets back so I could start breakfast, and I busied myself with piling pine needles and pine cones to get the fire started.

Brian was sixteen, tall and blonde, his fair skin suntanned from long hours outdoors, and Brett at thirteen was catching up quickly. Brett's brown hair curled close to his head, and he wasn't sure if he liked it that way. Brad had already had his eleventh birthday, and his sandy blonde hair had been lightened by the sun at this altitude of over eight thousand feet. People were always telling us that four-year-old Larissa looked just like her father with her dark brown hair and brown eyes.

I lifted the door on the luggage compartment to see what we had to cook. A wisp of wind blew the smoke from the fire back in my face, and I realized the wood was a little damp. We had flour, salt, baking powder, a little powdered milk and a jar of jelly. I looked for shortening or oil, but remembered we had used all of it the day before. We had saved some bacon grease, and I wondered how long it would keep without refrigeration—but the possibilities of pancake mix were there, so that's what we would have. Now should I have them put jelly on the pancakes or—maybe I could melt the jelly, add a little water, and make syrup—*grape syrup?* By the time they returned from their water trek, anything would look good!

I don't know how much time I spent worrying over how hard this was for them and how much we and the Lord were asking of them. Family and friends alike had warned us about taking our children away from home and its comforts, concerned that they would rebel and hate us for depriving them. But right now, I had time to read and study because they had a long walk ahead of them. The sun was melting the morning shadows and I had to squint to make out the words, *"Whoever desires to save his life will lose it, but whoever loses his life for my sake will find it."*(Matthew 16:25, author paraphrase)

The families who had come with us were visiting in a different area today. August was coming to a close, and school for the children was a looming question. What would the Lord have us do? We didn't know of a public school that was available, and somehow we sensed that sending them off to a boarding school was not the right answer either. I didn't even want to think about the onset of winter on the mountain yet.

Soon Don and the boys returned, enjoyed the pancakes, and looked forward to maybe getting biscuits for the evening meal. Problems surfaced here because our only cooking facility was a campfire, and I had no oven. How could we bake biscuits?

After breakfast, we took all the dirty dishes and placed them inside the bus, putting my big stew pot on the campfire to heat dishwater. If we left the dishes and pots outside, the local dogs would drag them away, and we didn't have any to spare.

Tom and Millie stopped by to visit, and we talked about biscuits. No problem! First, you build a campfire. While the wood is burning down to ashes, you prepare the biscuit dough and place the biscuits on a well-greased pan. Next, you grease one side of a paper grocery bag, dip it in water, and lay it greased side down on top of the biscuits. You shovel any burning wood away from the middle of the fire and bury the pan in the hot ash, being sure to shovel ashes on top of the brown bag covering the biscuits. In fifteen to twenty minutes you have a pan full of beautifully browned biscuits. It is necessary to be careful while removing the bag from the top so that you don't have ash-flavored biscuits.

Tom and Millie were the Navajo couple who first invited us to come up to Wheatfields and teach them. Millie was easy to talk to and always willing to translate the language for us or explain customs we were unfamiliar with. Her husband Tom was a hard working man whose wood-crafting skills continually amazed us. Tom had been in the Marines, worked as a heavy equipment operator, and had experience in rodeo. He was now the almost-reluctant pastor of the little church where we were teaching the people—reluctant not because he didn't want to pastor, but because he felt unqualified. A lot of the teaching we did was just answering questions for Tom privately and letting him present the answers to the people.

We learned a lot from them and from Millie's father Chee. I never had a conversation with him, not one where people talk about the weather, or the news, or the family. Our communications were different. Oh, they were real, but they were....

Well, I remember one morning on the mountaintop with wood smoke and cowboy coffee aromas drifting lazily past and the glow of the early morning sun sparkling through tall white pines. Off to my left, casual yet almost ethereal cotton candy clouds seemed for a moment trapped between the towering cliffs. What a contrast for someone like me, used to seeing clouds like marshmallow pillows high in the air, to look above the clouds and see elegant blue spruce and white pines reaching majestically for blue sky. For a moment I wanted to run over and touch them—these fluffy aliens that had dropped out of their heaven and into my world. They had my full attention as they began their graceful ascent—almost my full attention. The rhythmic sound of wood chopping had been very much a part of the morning when I stepped outside, but now my ears were stunned by the silence. Almost afraid to look away, fearing that the entire cloud scene would be gone, I glanced quickly toward the woodchopper. It was Millie's father, Chee.

The hands were gnarled and wrinkled, brown and glistening, almost reverently folded over the top of the axe handle. There was no sign of motion, not even the usual heavy breathing that comes automatically with the daily chore of bringing in firewood. The blue bandana knotted around his head and the plaid flannel shirt were his uniform. But now the nine decades that show plainly in the lined face and grey hair are nowhere visible in the eyes. The eyes reflect joy, an awesome glorious feeling that is inside me somewhere too, as we both watch until the last trace of mist is gone, and a busy day calls us to begin. He doesn't have to acknowledge that I am there. I am the white woman who invaded his world high in the Arizona mountains—the one who didn't know how to cook over open fires, and who gets huge blisters cutting wood and carrying water, the silly one who cries when perfectly natural things happen, like birthing babies. So now there is no wide grin, not even an almost smile, but a steady gaze in my direction and half a nod that says, "I'm glad you saw it too."

He is more than special, this Zuni Indian grandfather who speaks no English and has never been to school, who married into the Navajo tribe. Chee lives in a world where white men are strange and careless creatures who seldom learn his language and have little respect for the old ways. It's a world where medicine men call the shots, family is family, and hard work and heartaches are not an option. He is still amazed that my family should be there, these easterners accustomed to pushbutton living. Still, he teaches by doing, showing us how to start fires with a resin hardened wood that ignites instantly, and being patient when we choose the wrong wood and blacken our own faces with billowing puffs of smoke that look like tires burning. He has never suspected that white people and Indians might come to love each other. He's had no reason to.

Someday I would learn what a powerful impact Chee had already had on my life before we ever met.

CHAPTER 3

The Way Home

The summer was nearly gone, and we had experienced one day at a time the new world of trusting God for everything—food, clothing, medical care, safety. By this time, we had discovered some real faith—we thought. If we needed five dollars, we could pretty much expect it to come from somewhere.

One morning we assessed our needs for the day and decided there were a few things we needed. To start with, we'd like to have a main meal and some coffee. Milk would be a big help, and sugar, and somebody wanted Pop-Tarts. So we prayed and made our requests.

In an hour or so, a woman who spoke no English arrived at our campsite. Her broad smile meant the visit was a friendly one, and we stood observing each other for a few minutes. Her long skirt came just to the top of her socks, and her white tennis shoes showed very little of the dust from the walk up the hill. The velvet shirt was thin but still bright green, and her hair was tied in the traditional Navajo knot wrapped with yarn. We really didn't have any mirrors, and I wondered if I had black on my face from working with the morning fires. But now she was motioning that she wanted the boys to come with her.

They responded immediately, and the little procession left. I stood wondering—maybe she had some work for them to do. My curiosity was soon ended when they came back carrying a huge pot of mutton stew—our main meal for the day! She followed a long way behind, carrying a brown grocery bag. Smiling broadly, she handed it to us saying the Navajo word for bread. We understood that all morning she had been cooking stew and making fry bread for us.

Again, she motioned for someone to follow her, and back they came with a pot of coffee. We were so excited to know that some of our requests had been provided when another woman arrived. She spoke English, and wanted to know if we could use some extra milk she had, since she had no refrigeration and her children were away. *Yes*!

Main meal, coffee, and milk in less than two hours—three out of five things we had prayed for! We prayed again, thanking God for his answer to prayer, and prepared to eat. Opening the brown bag to take out the fry bread, we discovered a bag of sugar!

For some reason the Pop-Tarts never came—nevertheless, we were learning that God knew where we were.

Time moved quickly, and we began to be less of a curiosity. One of the missionary families moved down to Phoenix to help a daughter who was in great need, and shortly after, the air turned cold. The question of God's will for us had not yet been decided—would we stay here?—would we move on?—what about the winter? September arrived and tension began to mount.

The Navajo police came to bring Don a message—his father had a stroke and was very ill. Soon someone came from Gallup bringing a second message—Don's father, who had given his life to Jesus just three years before, was with the Lord. It was late in the day, and we held each other and asked God what to do—no money—no vehicle—no phone—sometimes the word responsibility rises without any clear-cut assignments. Don needed to be with his mother and sister and brother—they needed him, but how?

Soon the news spread through the area that Don's father had died, and Jonah came to drive us to Tsaile to find a telephone. (Jonah was the husband of Dorothy, the woman who brought us the mutton stew.) We had never been sure if Jonah welcomed us or regretted our presence on the mountain. He spoke no English, but stood beside us at the telephone offering a handful of coins. We were making the call collect, but his offer of help spoke volumes about his tender heart.

Someone in Ohio had collected about two hundred dollars toward getting us back the two thousand miles to the funeral. That would probably pay for the gasoline one way—if we had a car—but we didn't, and our attempts to borrow one didn't work either. Back at the bus, we climbed wearily into bed and silently talked to God. We would understand if he didn't want us to go, but we were asking him to let us be there. We knew it was impossible.

The next day we made a decision. If only Don could go, we'd try to arrange for that. We borrowed Tom and Millie's car to go to a telephone and call the airlines. Already we were having to use part of the collected money for gas. A ticket was available from New Mexico to Ohio for three hundred dollars. I called an old friend and told him what had happened. He said he would wire us three hundred dollars. The next step was to arrange for the flight—but we had missed one important piece of information. The plane would be leaving from Albuquerque, New Mexico, and we were in Wheatfields, Arizona. Don had no way to get to Albuquerque, which was over two hundred miles away. We felt as if we were under a dark smothering cloud and couldn't get out.

Brad had been coughing all day and had no appetite, and now that he had my attention, I noticed that he was burning up with fever. We were in Gallup, seventy miles from Wheatfields, and trying every possible avenue.

I called the bus terminal and asked how long it would take to get to Ohio. Three days—Don would miss the funeral.

Don said, "I don't feel good about going and leaving you and the children here alone. Let's see if we can get a bus ticket for the whole family, even if we don't make it for the service." One more phone call.

"Yes, ma'am, you can have the ticket for five hundred and twenty dollars if you can get a discount letter from the Catholic Church or some charity."

By this time we didn't have quite that much, counting what we'd already received and the three hundred dollars Paul was sending, with the expenses we'd already had just trying to work something out. Brad was leaning against the door, and when I touched him, I knew something had to be done, and soon.

We found the Catholic Charities office and asked the woman at the desk about the discount letter, expecting her to say it was only for Catholics. Instead she said there was no one there who could issue it, and we started to leave. "However," she said, "Our Lord told me to give you this." And she handed me a twenty-dollar bill.

It was late Wednesday night now, and Brad's condition had worsened. The funeral would be on Friday and there was no way anything could be done. We took Brad to the hospital where he received antibiotics, and we waited to know what to do next.

There was a bus leaving at one o'clock Thursday, so Thursday morning we again asked, "How much?"

"For six people, five hundred twenty dollars."

"No letter necessary?"

"No."

That meant we would be on the bus for three days with a sick child and no money for food. We asked our children what they wanted to do. They said, "We have crackers and a five-pound block of cheese. Let's do it!"

We were on the clock now. We had to pick up the three hundred dollars that had been wired, get the tickets, and catch the bus. When I got to Western Union I asked if they had a three hundred dollar wire for Don Cartwright.

"No, ma'am, we don't."

My heart sank. What could have happened to it? Surely, it would be there by now.

"But we do have a wire for Don Cartwright for five hundred dollars."

Rushing back to the bus station, I laid five hundred twenty dollars on the counter for the tickets. However, there was a different clerk on duty, who told us the tickets were one hundred nineteen dollars each. For six people that's seven hundred fourteen dollars. Finally he called someone who told him it was all right, and we were on our way.

The bus was so crowded we couldn't sit together, and Brad went to the back of the bus with Brian. I felt a tap on my shoulder and a young man said, "Get your kid away from me. I don't want to catch anything."

I understood that, but didn't know what to do. The only way to move him was to send our four-year-old to the back of the bus, and I knew she would be terrified of all those men.

Someone else offered to help us by changing seats, and I was able to sit with Brad and let him lean over on my lap to rest.

We arrived in Albuquerque and Don called his mother to let her know we wouldn't make it for the funeral, but we were coming. Then we learned that someone else had bought Don a ticket so that he could fly in from Oklahoma City. We would be in Oklahoma early Friday morning—he could get a taxi to the airport, and maybe, just maybe, he could be there before the funeral was over. I would arrive on the bus with our four children on Saturday.

Back on the bus, I turned and saw Brian and Brett involved in conversation with a tall man with a big beard who introduced himself as Jeremiah. He was fascinated by their stories of the mountaintop and the people there. He told us that his parents were in the ministry, and that he had been running from their prayers for years. He thought maybe meeting Brian, Brett, and Brad was a reminder from God that he "better get on the stick and make things right."

After the long night, we found ourselves pulling into a huge bus terminal in Oklahoma City. Don had no time to spare, and although I was glad he was going to get there, I hated to see him leave—I wasn't sure I could handle this by myself. Jeremiah had heard what was going on and assured me that he would help, and he did. We had a fast food breakfast and started back to the bus when Brad's face turned green and I saw him running down the long stairs to the restroom, hoping that he made it before he threw up!

The long grey bus was preparing to pull out and Brad was still in the men's restroom. I couldn't go in after him, and I hurried to ask the bus driver to please wait. He had problems of his own. An older white haired woman was involved in a heated discussion with him, and he was insisting she get off the bus. The driver was ranting and raving about "stupid foreigners that don't have any business in this country and should stay home."

Brian started talking to the woman, and I told the driver we needed time. The woman was from Denmark. She spoke English, but her accent was so strong that people couldn't understand her. Brian just mimicked her accent and they could communicate. She was terrified because she had spent eight thousand dollars on tickets for a tour of the United States—in her country you had a ticket for every stop, and she thought she was going to run out of tickets and be stranded. Brian and Brett were able to explain to her that this wasn't the case and everything was all right. She was so relieved!

We promised the bus driver that if he would give us five minutes we would take care of the woman and she wouldn't give him any more trouble. Brad arrived also much relieved, and so the woman from Denmark, Jeremiah, Brian, Brett, Brad, Larissa and I, along with the other passengers, began to settle in for the rest of the trip.

The woman behind us was traveling all the way to New Jersey with her little boy, who was busy teaching Larissa how to blow bubbles with bubble gum. Soon Jeremiah reached his stop, and as he left the bus, we gave him our Bible. We had written him a letter telling him how much we appreciated him and assuring him that God loves him very dearly and has a plan for his life. We placed the letter in the Bible in the book of Jeremiah.

As the afternoon wore on, we were all feeling the effects of the heat. The bus driver stopped at a Dairy Queen. The woman from Denmark asked permission to buy the children ice cream cones. Larissa enjoyed that chocolate cone. Her dress got more of it than she did!

Meanwhile, Don was arriving at the airport in Columbus, Ohio, where his brother-in-law, Jack, met him and drove furiously to the cemetery. The funeral service had ended and everyone was gathered at the cemetery when he arrived. There were no dry eyes as the car door flew open and Don ran, just in time to see his dad's face one more time, and to thank God for the precious man who had stood with us around the coffee table and prayed that God would bless Don and his family in the work they were called to.

Brad was beginning to feel a little better, but we still had another evening and a long night to spend on the bus, sitting up. Saturday morning the Greyhound pulled into the terminal in Columbus, and Don met us there.

What was the next step? Did God have a plan, or were we on our own? There was no money and no way to get back—and what were we going back to?—a mountaintop in the frozen winter, a bus with beds but no kitchen or heat, and no income. What exactly were we to do?

The answer was not spoken, but somehow we felt it. *You take care of today and God will take care of tomorrow.*

There were people to comfort, encourage, and pray for.

Dorothy and Jonah Descheene

The blue bus with brush arbor beside it for shade

Meeting at brush arbor shelter to distribute goods

CHAPTER 4

A Pile of Suns

Columbus, Ohio—what a different world with all its hustle and bustle and people milling about in the bus terminal! Don and his mother were there to pick us up. We didn't have much luggage to worry about, so we were quickly on our way—just a few days of seeing family and old friends—and then what?

I refused to let my mind dwell on "then what?" As difficult as it had been to get to Ohio, how would we ever get back to the Reservation?

We were asked to speak at Don's mother's church, and they gave us over two hundred dollars. Our good friends Paul and Edna Sullivan invited us to visit and wanted to know what we needed most. The answer was easy—any kind of vehicle! A van would be wonderful. My mother was letting us use her car to get around while we were there.

So Paul and Edna began to pray that the Lord would use them. God had ministered to us through them so many times in the past that we were a little embarrassed to let them do it again. Once during the summer as we traveled around the Navajo Reservation our funds had completely dried up. We were over two hundred miles from the place where we got our mail, and things were getting very hard. Bernice, one of the Navajo women who had been our interpreter and was so kind to us, had offered to take us to the post office. Don prayed, "Lord, if you want us to continue this ministry there will be money in that mailbox. If there is not, we will quit now."

I hadn't had the nerve to pray that way, and I waited on pins and needles to see what the mailbox held. Hardly anyone was communicating with us and we often found the mailbox empty after a drive of many miles.

Don came back with an envelope. Inside was a letter from Paul and Edna, and one line of that letter was a whole letter from God to us. She wrote, "My nudger (Holy Spirit) will not leave me alone until I send this, so must mail it right away." The letter contained a check for four hundred dollars!

Now we were back in Ohio, and again they were saying, "We want to help." And help they did! Paul found a 1976 GMC Suburban, five years old and in excellent shape. He bought it and equipped it with tires. Edna and others started filling it up with food, clothing, books, and old magazines that would later become very important to us. Paul also gave us his generator, and by the end of October, we were on our way back to the Reservation.

By the time we got back to New Mexico, we discovered that the other family we were working with had decided to start pastoring a Navajo church about one hundred twenty miles from where we were. We were on our own.

Winding up the mountain road, we noticed something that resembled powdered laundry detergent on both sides of the pavement. It took another half mile for us to realize that it was snow! The thoughts racing through my mind were not comforting.

Facing winter at eight thousand feet altitude—no real home—only a bus with beds and nothing else—no heat, no kitchen, no water, no electricity—strange culture, strange language—witchcraft, prejudice—would we even be welcome? No job, no income,—no place to even get a job—four children, the youngest only four years old—Thanksgiving coming, Christmas coming—

My mind shut down.

One word began to echo over and over—*Trust. Trust. Trust…*

A cool wind blew ripples in the water of the lake as we passed by. The water's edge came up to the road, and we knew we were almost there. Turning onto the dirt road, we were all anxious to know what God had in store for us.

The big blue bus was still there. One or two things were missing—we had rigged an awning of sorts out of a sheet to give a little shade, and someone had taken it down. Soon our natural instincts took over and we began to unpack our supplies and make the bus feel usable again. Fear and anxiety were strangely absent, but questions were surfacing.

In the morning Tom and Millie noticed we were back and came to see what our plans were. In the Navajo culture it is considered rude to come directly to the point—you must first visit and make small talk, and much later you bring up the real subject. We had no idea what they were going to say. They might easily say they wanted us to leave, and if they did, we would go. But the things they were talking about didn't really sound that way. Were we interested in going out to get wood with them?

Finally, Tom in his quiet way spoke from his heart. "I do not know much about the Bible. We need to learn, and we have tried to understand, but the words are hard. Do you think you can stay here and teach us for a little time, or must you go somewhere else?"

Then Millie spoke. "We joined a denomination and asked them to send teachers, but they don't have enough teachers to send. If we don't learn, our church will die."

Having promised God—and them—that we would do all we could do, we set about the task of making our little mountaintop home livable. It was strangely comfortable there on our bus with just beds and now a little Coleman camp stove. Early in the morning, Don would get up, light the stove and put on coffee or tea, and by the time the sun came up, the air would be just warm enough. If we had lots of fuel, I would cook breakfast on the two burners; if not, we'd build a campfire outside and watch the early morning clouds lift. We knew that soon we would have to find a way to cook inside, because Thanksgiving, harbinger of winter, was just days away.

It was getting colder, and snow was blowing across the roof and melting in the smoke from the chimney of the little church. The rickety little benches and makeshift chairs formed a new pattern now, closer to the stove. The stove was an old army water-can, sitting on its side on metal legs. A hole had been cut in one side for a stovepipe, and the end had been cut off and hinged with wire so that wood could be loaded in. The fire felt good.

The wind was pressing its way into the little building, blowing the curtains until they were almost horizontal. These weren't ordinary curtains. We had been given some hand-embroidered albs once used in a Catholic church and discarded when they became too worn for use. They were embroidered with crosses, wheat, grapes, and many other symbols of the church. As they began to ravel, we cut off the worn parts and made "elegant" curtains for this little Navajo church with its dirt floor.

The people were coming in—slowly, oblivious to the modern watches that some wore on their wrists. Chester, faithful as ever, was the first one there. His hearing was not good, and his smile created a welcome attitude for a Sunday morning service. Elizabeth was making her way up the path; Marie, Jonah, and Dorothy were right behind her. A little girl about four years old darted quickly inside the door, and just as quickly was gone. After Tom, Millie, and a few others arrived, we had thirty-two people for the service.

About two weeks earlier, we had been asked to begin teaching the Bible as though we were teaching kindergarten children right from the beginning—but how? We thought about it and realized that most Bible-teaching involves words or preaching. Many of the words used by evangelists—justification, sanctification, revelation, prophecy, propitiation, crucifixion, inhabitants, anointing, thee, thou, chastisement—had no meaning to the people. The Navajos are people who understand pictures, and their language is a very descriptive one. For instance, the Navajo word for "airplane" is translated "car that flies" and the word for "helping" is translated "for each other."

We had very little to work with. We stretched a wire across the front of the church on two nails and pinned a blanket to the wire. Armed with straight pins from the sewing box and a few pictures we cut from old Reader's Digest advertisements, we looked for a place to begin.

We needed something to describe creation, so this morning we started teaching Genesis with two yellow plastic margarine bowls, a blue-and-green Christmas tree ornament, and a tiny white Styrofoam ball.

Most people we knew had studied the solar system in school, and knew all about the orbits of the earth and moon, but many of our Navajo friends had never been to school. So now Don inverted one yellow margarine bowl on top of the other and stood in one place representing the sun, while Brian carried the blue-and-green tree ornament representing the earth and walked around Don, demonstrating the earth's path. Everyone laughed as Brad, with the little white Styrofoam moon, tried to walk around Brian while Brian orbited Don. Eventually they all understood Genesis 1:14-

18 and God's system of giving us night and day and seasons. We asked if there were any questions.

Mostly smiles—but slowly Grandfather Chee's hand went up and he began to speak in Navajo. Tom translated his words.

"I want to thank you for telling me the truth. All my life I get up every morning and watch the path of the sun across the sky. It starts low and cool and rises high and makes great heat. Then as night comes, it falls into the western sky and leaves a great glow. I thought it was a different sun that crossed the sky each day and fell into a pile, making a big fire. I am so happy to know that God has a better way, and I want to thank you for coming to tell us about it."

Inside church at Wheatfields, AZ showing wood stove

Church at Wheatfields showing the "elegant" curtains (also note baby on a cradleboard in woman's lap below window)

CHAPTER 5

What Is Thanksgiving?

In mid-November, wood chopping became a vital part of every day's activities, and wood gathering preceded that event with lots of prayer on my part. Sending young boys into the mountains with an axe and a chainsaw that sometimes worked required mountains of faith for me. Don and our sons had labored with Tom through the summer, helping him build his house with just those tools—an axe and a chainsaw. Tom and his family had been living in a tent when we came, and they really needed to get their house under roof before winter.

One day I began to see that I was probably just too female and unadventurous when I observed part of this wood-gathering process. Brian, Brett, and Brad had discovered a huge log that would require several hours to cut up and carry back to the bus, and it was almost dark. They thought it through and decided to chain it to the Suburban and drag it back to cut up. I understood that reasoning—but then I heard loud yelling and looked to see what the problem was. The Suburban was traveling slowly up the road with the gigantic log chained to the back. The yelling sounded like a bull rider—"Yee hah!"

The log had riders! The boys were standing upright on the log that was being towed like triumphant cowboys, totally oblivious to the shock waves going through their mother's mind at the thought of what could happen if they fell!

As the day before Thanksgiving arrived, I tried not to think about Thanksgivings of the past. I was not successful. The last dinner I had prepared for several of our relatives was a very special one. We lived in a three-story townhouse with white carpet, and I spent weeks getting ready for the event. I had grapevine wreaths with copper ornaments on the walls and a white lace tablecloth over an apricot liner with chocolate-colored napkins and accents on the table. The centerpiece was beautiful, the table settings elegant. We had pumpkin pies made from scratch, Don's favorite lemon meringue pie, and of course my mom's famous bread pudding, along with oyster dressing, cranberry sauce, homemade noodles, two turkeys, homemade yeast rolls, Don's mom's strawberry angel, and too many other dishes to fit on the counters. After it was all over, the dishes went into the dishwasher and we gathered around to sing hymns and talk about fun times of the past.

There were similarities—we did have a turkey, and Thanksgiving was coming on the appropriate November Thursday.

As we rushed through our evening meal and prepared for the Wednesday evening service, I wondered again how I could cook the turkey. In the past, I just prepared the turkey, put it in the oven, and then set the temperature and timer. But now we were cooking all of our meals over an open campfire, and the only solution I could see was to boil it in a big pot. We could arrange it on some kind of spit to roast and then keep someone there to fend off wild animals and dogs—even boiling it would require constant watching.

The families were arriving now for church. We were beginning to learn that "seven o'clock church" never seemed to be at seven o'clock. In the summer it was always an hour or two later. In the winter it could be an hour or two earlier. It gave new meaning to the scripture, *"Be instant in season, out of season."* (2 Timothy 4:2)

Eventually, we discovered that church would probably start at "dark-thirty," or half an hour past dark. That made sense because the people are shepherds—they brought in their sheep just before dark, had their meal, and then came to church. Many white missionaries had tried and failed to change this practice, preaching about being faithful to God by being on time for church—and then dealing with frazzled nerves when the people came early or showed up after the service, expecting another sermon. We decided that if we really wanted to reach the people, the answer was for us to change and follow their schedule.

We opened with the customary prayer, and I really didn't know what time it was. Starting the singing with the chorus, "This Is the Day," I noticed that some of the people were clapping their hands completely out of rhythm, so I began to teach them how to clap on the beat, exaggerating the motion to help them learn. Someone came up to the front and asked if we could come outside to pray for a person who was in their car and not feeling well. We left the building and prayed, and then came back in. The people were laughing so hard we didn't know what was happening. One of the church grandfathers was up front pretending to be me, leading the singing and doing the same exaggerated clapping motions I had done. He stopped suddenly when he saw me, and everything got quiet.

I could tell by their faces that no one wanted me to feel insulted, and they were afraid that I had been. My imitator, Jonah, sat down. He didn't speak English, so I went over to the log he was sitting on and motioned for him to stand up. I took his arm and led him to the front, and we started the song again. Stepping down in front of him, I made sure he was watching and then began to do the same motions again, gesturing for him to join me. When they saw me laugh and knew that it was all right, everyone began to sing and clap with all their might. We sang that song over and over until everyone collapsed in peals of laughter. The clapping improved greatly after that.

Darkness settled in, and the lantern didn't offer much illumination. Leading the singing was fairly easy because I didn't have to read the words, but I didn't know how Don and Tom would read the Bible. Someone opened the back door and a cold blast of air accompanied him into the room. Then something caught my attention on the back wall—I was astonished to see a whole row of baby smiles looking back at me! There were several large nails in the wall, and hanging from them were babies in cradleboards, enjoying the service from their lofty perch. It took a minute for us to recover our composure after seeing them.

These cradleboards were made of redwood, and consisted of two flat boards angled at the top and attached by leather lacing to each other, with a small footrest. A large curved bow protected the baby's head if the cradleboard ever fell over, and the baby was wrapped snugly in a blanket that was also laced to the board with leather. The babies were absolutely content to be wrapped securely in their cradleboards and lined up along the wall where they could see over everyone else's heads!

The service was soon over, and Elizabeth came up to shake my hand. (Hugging just wasn't done among these Navajos who had been taught that you get evil spirits from touching white people, but we had progressed some.) Elizabeth was a large woman with a beautiful smile that her whole face got into, and she did not speak English. We knew that she wanted something, and had to ask Millie what it was. Millie said, "She wants to take your turkey."

God Knows Where I Am

Our turkey! That was all we had to make it Thanksgiving! Well, Lord, I guess we'll give her our turkey. And go to bed. And wonder what next.

What will we have tomorrow? What will we tell the children?

The sun came up late, and at first I thought I'd just wait for it to shine brightly before getting out of bed. This just wasn't Thanksgiving Day—no special table settings—not even a table—no special cooking aromas, no kitchen hustle and bustle—no kitchen—no family coming over, no Macy's Parade on television, no big football game on television—no television! It was just another day.

Brian, Brett, and Brad were already up building the fire, and little Larissa was asking, "What is Thanksgiving? Who started it? Do they have it in heaven? Why do you eat on Thanksgiving?"

Feeling a little annoyed with all the questions, I felt a nudge from the Lord. "Aren't you going to answer the child's questions?"

"Do I have to?"

Nothing but silence, even in my own heart.

The first question floated across my mind like a plane carrying a sign behind it:

"What is Thanksgiving?"

Well, it's being thankful.

"For what?"

For everything, I guess. The first celebration was to thank God for their survival through difficult times, and the harvest.

"Do they have it in heaven? Why do you eat? What did they eat?"

Whatever they had.

"Thankful to whom?"

To God and each other.

"Who started it?"

The Indians and people who came to tell them about the Lord.
Really?
Like a printer spilling out pages of words my thoughts tumbled over the hundreds of ways my family and I had been blessed by the Lord—protected, provided for, and given favor. None of us was sick, and we had this unique opportunity to share this special time with the Navajos in Arizona's mountains. Quickly I checked through our food supply to see what I could make. There were mashed potatoes, green beans, some squash, and biscuits. I had some cocoa powder, and was reminded of something my aunt used to make when I was a little girl. We sometimes went to visit her in the Blue Ridge Mountains of Virginia, and we all hurried to her breakfast table for fried apples and this treat. Everybody called it chocolate gravy, and she served it with hot buttered biscuits. I knew it sounded strange, but I also remembered that we had all loved it! Not quite as rich and sweet as chocolate pudding, it was a chocolate sauce made by adding cocoa powder and sugar to a white-sauce mix, and it was a wonderful accompaniment to homemade biscuits.

We were all amazed at how festive we felt with the smell of fall and drifting leaves and wood smoke in the air, and that slight nippy feel of cold weather coming soon. Everybody wanted to stir or chop or slice or do anything to be a part of the preparations and excitement of making it Thanksgiving: *"Do everything that you do heartily, as unto the Lord..."* (Colossians 3:23, author paraphrase)

Thanksgiving doesn't come in a package of things you must have. It comes out of your heart when you are grateful for what's already there and begin to look and see what God has blessed you with that you did not even realize you had.

Not knowing what time the dinner and the service were to be, we just decided to be ready. Soon little boys and girls began to arrive, some carrying small dishes and brown paper bags filled with Navajo fry bread and tortillas. Teenagers showed up with mutton stew, punch, soft drinks, and fruit salad. There was even a pot of Navajo tea. And then something completely wonderful happened! The aroma of roast turkey floated across the mountaintop preceding the arrival of our own holiday turkey, fully, tenderly and moistly cooked in Elizabeth's huge outdoor dirt oven along with seven others. She knew that I was perplexed about how to roast the turkey. They had built a huge dirt mound, hollowed it out, built a fire inside, and then shoveled out the fire. The turkeys were placed in it, the door was sealed, and at the proper time the roasted poultry was removed, ready to serve!

"*In every thing give thanks, for this is the will of God concerning you...*"! (1 Thessalonians 5:18)

Elizabeth's dirt oven that baked the turkey

Cooking in dirt oven

Inside the Wheatfields Church. See the nails along the back wall with coats where the cradleboard babies hung.

The elegant curtains—also note baby on cradleboard

Cradleboard

Making a cradleboard

Cradleboard hanging on Mission wall

Chapter 6

Tell Me the Story of Jesus

December—the Christmas month—the giving month—the family month—arrived on schedule, and home was still the big blue school bus. There had been no further instruction from the Lord, and we still had no visible means of support. Parts from our bus engine had been in the shop for some time when finally a small tax refund arrived making it possible for us to pick them up, but we still needed other parts which were unavailable. My brother and his family from Ohio came to visit, and then decided to go on down to Phoenix, away from the snow and bad roads.

In years past we had often directed a Christmas play for our church, so we asked if the Wheatfields families would like to have a Christmas play. After long explanations of what a Christmas play was, the answer was yes.

We had no idea of the creative and artistic abilities of Tom and Millie Begay's family—soon Tom was happily involved in decorating the front of the church. He draped fresh cedar across the front, and on each side used a small tree to give the effect of a greenery frame. We also had a strand of twinkle lights, and if there was gas available for the generator, sometimes we could light them up.

Rehearsals started. It was to be the simple story of the birth of Jesus. We began with Millie playing a mother telling her child the story of Christmas, and our son Brad sitting at her feet playing her child. Just before she began the story, teen girls carrying candles and dressed in their traditional Navajo dress marched in singing "Tell Me the Story of Jesus" in Navajo. Then as Millie told about each happening, the shepherds came, the angels sang, and Mary and Joseph welcomed all, along with their new baby. Someone made cardboard cutouts of sheep and stood them up on the stage for the rehearsals.

We had several practice evenings, and were surprised to see the whole community come to every practice. We tried to explain that these were just rehearsals and the main event would occur the Sunday before Christmas. We didn't understand that they were excited just to have something going on, and they came every day to see the decorations and experience the holiday fun.

Finally, it got so cold that we began sleeping in the church at night, and I wondered what we would do for our family Christmas. We had a few dollars for food, and made a trip to Gallup to get some supplies and just a little of the atmosphere of the holiday. Brad had some change, and he went into a store and bought a small amount of bulk chocolate chips. He planned to give them as gifts, but somehow in the rush of the evening he lost them. Brett and Brian bought a little gift box of cheese for us. My brother and his wife had come from Ohio to visit and brought a big gift-wrapped box of cookies for our children. I stashed it on the bus, so I knew we would have that. We could manage.

The Saturday morning before the play we were awakened early by a knock on the door. The young man standing there in the snow was wearing no shirt and no shoes, just jeans and a vest. He was obviously very drunk, and informed us that he had just been "rolled." His paycheck, boots, shirt, and ID had all been taken. Immediately our hearts dropped for his wife and children who were waiting for him to come home so they could get food for the family.

As difficult as the situation was, he was a comical figure, trying to explain that his biggest problem was the loss of his identification. "Without my ID I don't know if I'm a... Navajo Indian...or a....Hopi Indian...or a White Indian. But I gotta get...home....They'll know...who I am....How I gonna get my car...back home?"

Brian and Don volunteered to drive him to his house. Brian could drive his car and Don would follow to bring Brian back.

"But how you gonna...get my...car back home?"

Instructions were repeated. Of course, the mushy, slippery roads were a concern for me, but the decision was made. Again the question came.

"But how you gonna...get my car back?"

And again the answer came, "Drive it!"

"But...I...flew it in here!"

After seeing the condition of the road, Brian said he must have been right. They didn't see how a man in his inebriated condition could possibly have driven on good roads, much less the ones they traveled to get him home!

The last rehearsal before the play came, and when the signal was given for the angels to enter, only our little Larissa and three-year-old Tami Begay were there. The teen girls did not come in, so we stopped the rehearsal with the question "Where are the angels?"

A voice answered "They're on top of the bus, gambling!" The whole place broke up in laughter and we ran outside to see that indeed the girls were sitting on top of the bus playing cards (although they weren't gambling). They scrambled down to take their positions as angels.

Since we had no costumes for them, I used some long fabric pieces I had for makeshift costumes. Larissa's costume was a white pillowcase that we opened at the top seam and pinned at the shoulders—after the play, we could sew it back together and use it again for pillows. We started the same kind of costume for Tami, but she refused to be a "White angel." So she wore her Navajo traditional clothes, long velvet skirt and velvet top with a woven sash, and she made a very pretty Navajo angel.

The evening of the play arrived along with some snow, and the place was full—inside and out! The little cardboard sheep were lovely, but they couldn't compete with the real live baby goats the shepherds were carrying! And these were real live shepherds coming to the stable to celebrate the birth of Jesus. It was such joy for us to be a part of this. Hearing the girls sing "Tell Me the Story of Jesus" in Navajo brought a flood of thankful tears.

Now that the play was finished, we could concentrate on the family Christmas celebration. I would rewrap the box of cookies into individual packages so everyone would have something to open, and the boys could wrap their cheese gift.

A sudden noise caught my attention, and I heard people yelling outside. Brad came in to tell me that some dogs had forced open the door of the bus and taken the cheese and cookies. We hurried outside and saw the pieces of paper strewn across the hillside.

Monday morning brought little encouragement for a Christmas holiday with our family. Someone had scheduled a Christmas revival at the little Wheatfields church, and it would run through to the New Year. The evangelist was someone we did not know, and all the sermons would be in Navajo. The revival began, and every evening the service would start about dark and continue until two or three in the morning. We did not know what was being said, but we had an uneasy feeling about it.

Christmas Eve arrived and we didn't quite know what to do. In our family, that had always been a special time. Sometimes we attended a candlelight service, or we had an open house for family and friends. The tree and house would be decorated with every decoration we could think of, and Scripture read. Homemade fudge, divinity and all sorts of other Christmas delicacies would be spread out for all to enjoy, their aromas filling the air. Last minute secrets about gifts would be shared, and as each family stopped by, they would stuff a bag with presents labeled for each of their children. We usually had one or two extra, generic gifts on hand in case someone unexpected showed up. We made homemade eggnog and punch and hot chocolate, and watched for snowflakes to make it a white Christmas.

We teased each other about what was, or was not, in the packages. One year Brian discovered a tapestry of a huge elk that he asked us to get him for Christmas. So we told him that while we were standing at the counter waiting to purchase it, a woman handed money to the clerk and bought it. What we didn't tell him was that I was that woman!

But now it was the exciting hour, Christmas Eve, and there wasn't even a place to sit down inside out of the cold. The evangelist preached on and on, shouting until she was hoarse; children wandered in and out, and people who were afraid of offending God on his special holiday tried to pay attention.

Our four-year-old was begging to go to bed, but it was too cold on the bus, and the service still wore on. Finally, when we were too tired to do anything else, it was over. Everyone left, and we went to bed. It was good that we were so tired, because my mind could not be overrun with thoughts of what we would do for Christmas morning. What would we do? There were no gifts, no relatives coming and no special dishes to prepare.

We didn't wake up early. Don built the fire and we found something for breakfast. I wrote out gift certificates promising things for future times. I promised to make each a special shirt. We promised to take Brian to Gallup to get his temporary driving permit and then let him drive all the way back. And as we did every Christmas, Don turned in the Bible to the Christmas story from Luke and read, "*And it came to pass in those days, that there went out a decree from Caesar Augustus, that all the world should be taxed...*" (Luke 2:1)

I listened to the words I'd heard so many times before. Mary and Joseph hadn't expected their first Christmas to be like that either. They didn't even know it was a Christmas. I'm sure that Mary had hoped to be at home with her mother and family when her baby was born, not in a stable in an unfamiliar place. And then the baby *was* born, and all the familiar things of home were missing. But Joseph was there. Mary was there. Jesus was there.

The room began to take on a warm glow as I looked around at Tom's cedar tree decorations, the log benches, the Bible in Don's hand, and Brian, Brett, Brad, and Larissa. The presence of God was so rich that I couldn't find anything lacking. It was Christmas, and Jesus really was the gift of all gifts.

"*...and the glory of the Lord shone round about them...*" he continued to read. Verse 17 says, "*And when they had seen it, they made known abroad the saying which was told them concerning the child.*" That was our job, making known the great love of God that he was willing to send his only Son, and that his only Son was willing to come.

We exchanged our certificates. Don had a little combination nail clipper with a small knife blade as a gift for me, and it proved to be a very useful tool for all of us in the months to come. I expected disappointment, but instead saw a spirit of adventure and joy in being together on a mission for Jesus. If he could give up heaven and come to earth for us, surely we could do this for him.

The angels enter the church for Christmas pageant.

Wheatfields Church Christmas pageant

Tom and Millie Begay with goats for Christmas pageant and the two littlest angels, Tami Begay and Larissa Cartwright

Youth in traditional dress

CHAPTER 7

Watch What You Discard

The revival was finally over, and we were part of the services again. Snow just happened—every day, almost. One evening we prepared for the service and I diligently swept the little dirt floor, causing everything to be coated with dust. Elizabeth, who spoke no English, stood at the open door and watched. Finally, she came and took the broom out of my hand, placing it against the wall. Then she slipped back out the door. Before I had a chance to know what she meant by that, she came back in with hands full of snow. Sprinkling snow all over the floor, she put the broom back in my hands. Voila! No flying dust!

We put the little broken chairs and log benches back in place, and others began to come in. Joe and Elsie found their place, and put a big bag down on one of the chairs. They had walked six miles in the snow to come to church. Joe smiled and pointed to the bag. "Bear sign."

Bear sign? Their word for the homemade doughnuts they had made for us and carried the whole six miles!

Tom was bringing the message this evening. He began by describing his time in Viet Nam and talking about the importance of carefully choosing the words we speak. He reminded us of the words in the Bible, *"Out of the abundance of the heart the mouth speaketh..."* (Matthew 12:34)

In Viet Nam, many of the Marines had battery operated small appliances, radios, razors and flashlights. When the batteries were dead, new ones were installed and the old ones thrown in the trash. One day they noticed their trash was disappearing.

"No problem—if the enemy wants to steal our trash that's less for us to worry about—doing us a favor."

Many new booby traps started showing up, things designed to trap and injure and harass the young marines. Each was set off by a small electrical charge, a charge coming from a string of "dead" batteries wired together. There was just enough power left in them to activate the traps. Their own discards were hurting them! Tom now made the comparison, "What are your carelessly used words doing? Are they being turned into weapons against you that Satan can use?"

It was a long time before sleep came that night. *Lord, who is teaching whom?—and six miles in the snow!*

By this time, we were firmly entrenched in winter's icy grip. Snow was a common occurrence, and getting in and out became more difficult. One evening we were asked to come to a church service in a hogan in the Tsaile area, and after church one of the families needed a ride home. As we started out across the desert, we quickly realized that snow had obliterated any sign of which way the road went. Often people made new trails, especially when the usual paths became impassable—and you had to be a native of the area to know which way to go in *good* weather. On this fifteen-mile trek, you just had to pray. Soon the snow had drifted, and it was blowing straight across the bug shield of the Suburban into the windshield, and we were pushing a path through the snow. When we finally arrived at their hogan and the passengers got out, I was thoroughly lost. Don has an excellent sense of direction, however, and somehow we made it back to the main highway.

Snow dropped heavily Friday morning, and the afternoon was cold and windy when Elizabeth and her father came to ask if we could go to the boarding school at Many Farms to bring her daughters and their laundry home for the weekend. Many families in Wheatfields saw their children only when they had a way to get home from the boarding schools, and Elizabeth and her father had no vehicle. The boarding school was in a town about forty miles away. We would be able to go to a grocery store—there was enough money on hand to buy flour, oatmeal and maybe a few other things. When we got there, we found that her girls were experiencing flu symptoms and some fever.

Soon we were on our way back, but the heavy snowfall of that day had melted on top and then frozen again, making a glass-like covering over everything. When we reached the turn to go up our mountain road, the wheels started spinning and we weren't going anywhere. After about thirty minutes, we knew we had a long, cold walk ahead of us.

Taking everything we thought we could carry, we locked the Suburban and quickly pulled our coats close to us. Thank God for the moon. It would light our way and we wouldn't have to carry a lantern. We were quite a procession. Elizabeth's father was in his eighties, and we were probably more concerned than he was.

I can't remember having such a fear of falling before. The narrow ruts in the snow were wide enough if each step were carefully placed, and yet in my hurry, balance seemed to elude me. I couldn't feel my nose stinging in the cold now, and instinctively I wanted to touch it to see if I could feel it at all. My hands were too full; I couldn't let go. Ice crystals reflected moonlight on top of the snow and in the towering trees, like diamonds flung across the frozen earth. How I could enjoy that if we were safe inside with a roaring fire.

Fire—where did I put the matches?
What if this was one of the times we couldn't get the fire to start?
Strange—the wind is blowing, yet the moon is still bright. Am I awake or is this just a nightmare?
I could have felt sorry for us, but then I remembered the children who were making this walk with flu symptoms.

I looked back to see where the boys were. Far behind me, I could see three figures plodding a step at a time, pushed back by the bitter wind. The one in the middle plunged forward and was righted as the others grabbed for him. It was Elizabeth's father with Brian and Brett. My conscience panged as I saw their hands uncovered trying to hold the old man up and prevent a serious fall. They could have run ahead, taking advantage of the strength of their youth and their long legs, but they would not leave him.

Lord, where was the money we should have had to buy warm gloves and boots for them? Was my faith at fault?
Don and Brad had stopped, stamping their frozen feet in the ice as they exchanged burdens. Four-year-old Larissa and two bags of groceries were traded to ease the strain on tired muscles. Beside me, Elizabeth's big brown eyes riveted on the light ahead; she pushed on, laundry basket swaying from side to side.

I knew my feet were wet, and the stinging was beginning to subside. Two miles in sub-zero weather even on level ground would have been difficult, and this was up hill all the way. With half a mile to go, a feeling of desperation swept over me. What if one of us had frostbite? What would we do?

I prayed for extra strength and began to run. I fell once, twice, a third time, and twisted my ankle. Staying in the ruts was so difficult, but if we tried to walk outside the ruts, the layer of ice might crack and we'd sink deep into the snow. I decided to try walking on top of the frozen snow, and found that it was hard enough to support my weight—*good!*

God Knows Where I Am

I could see the tiny building in the distance now.

If I hurry, one foot in front of the other—hurry—I can get a fire started and have it warming by the time the others get there.

I didn't have as much to carry as they did. The wind was blowing harder now, and the snow-crystal diamonds had disappeared. It must be about one o'clock.

I put my right hand inside my jacket to insure that I could use it when I got inside.

Inside—what a nice warm feeling that word had!

At last—the door!

Struggling to remove the wood stick from the hasp, I dropped my load.

That's okay. I'm here. The door is open. Now to find the matches in the dark. I remember—in the window, on the sill.

Feeling in the right corner, I found one packet. I lit the first one.

Only six matches—got to make it count. There are pine needles and pine cones in the wood box—one tissue in my pocket—that will do.

I struck a match, then another and another—still no fire. Three matches left. Outside I could hear them coming.

"Smoke! That means fire! Praise the Lord!"

Dropping bundles and pulling off shoes at the same time, they fell on the floor and I counted to make sure they were all there. The others walked on another two hundred yards, anxious for the comfort of their own fire.

We broke the ice in the water barrel and put a few chunks in the coffee pot. In a few minutes we had almost dry clothes, coffee, and leftover fry bread. Not considered small pleasures any more, these were great treasures.

When we were assured that there was no frostbite, we breathed a prayer of thanksgiving for our safety and pulled out the bedrolls. Don and I worried that the fire would go out while we were sleeping, but we were too exhausted to stay

awake. We covered the children with everything we could find, including the dirty laundry.
Dirty laundry? Am I really doing this?
But sleep was quickly calling me and I didn't need any courage or convictions right now.

Joe and Elsie Begay who made bear sign (doughnuts) and walked six miles in snow to deliver them shown standing under a rainbow with Lynn and Larissa Cartwright

CHAPTER 8

For Each Other

It was Saturday evening and we had just heated water on the stove to wash dishes. As soon as that chore was done, we would heat more water to shampoo hair and try sponge baths to prepare for the Sunday service. We tried to get the Grand Junction, Colorado, station on the radio because they had a story hour we enjoyed, and it was relaxing at times. We were just a little on edge because this week we had received a visit from the area director for the denomination that had assumed responsibility for the little church. He had decided that it might be best if we did not stay here any longer. His personal viewpoint was that white people should not live on the Reservation, and should limit their activities there to a few days at a time. We tried to explain our position, knowing that it would be nearly impossible to make anyone understand what was happening unless they too lived with the people. Nevertheless, we felt keenly the problem of being submissive to God and to the human authority in that situation.

We also discovered that there was one local family who delighted in stirring up problems, and they had made negative reports to the church director.

As we struggled with this and silently prayed for an answer, there was a knock on the door. We opened it and Millie's teenage son stumbled through. His face was bloody and torn, and the front of his shirt was ripped and dripping also. We looked through our meager first aid supply and found only a small amount of hydrogen peroxide and a piece of gauze.

We took some of the water being heated for dishes and cooled it down to wash his face and see how serious the injuries were.

"What happened?"

Brian, Brett, and Brad tried to get him to talk. He was very shy and the words were few.

"Nobody would let me in!"

"What do you mean?" I asked.

He put his hands on his head and bent forward. I thought he was going to throw up.

"They tried to throw me out of the car. They opened the door and shoved me out, but just my face hit the ground, and they kept going."

We finally understood that he had been out with some of his friends who were drinking. They tried to throw him out of the car, but his feet remained tangled inside and his face dragged the ground before he fell completely out. Then he walked for almost fifteen miles trying to get help. He kept knocking on doors, but when people saw his bloody face, their superstition and fear would not let them help him.

We did all that we could for him and then our boys walked down to tell his parents what had happened.

There was a tent revival going on at the same time, and the next morning no one came to church. We waited and prayed, and after a few minutes Tom, Millie and their daughter Tami walked in the door. We could see that they were very upset. As usual, we had to wait a while for them to say what the problem was.

The story had gotten out that rather than a teen-age boy who had been dragged on his face, we had received an injured drunk man into the church building the night before, and that was taboo.

The leader at the tent revival had prophesied to all the people that God was very displeased with us for defiling the church, and they should not go back there until the evangelist went in and cleansed it of the demons. If they did go, their children would die.

We looked at Tom and Millie and felt the heavy weight they bore. Here they were with their precious little girl, torn between their fears of disobeying the evangelist, the possible death of their children, and their appreciation to us for helping their son. They hadn't known us long enough to know which Christian was telling them the truth. Was God truly angry with us for taking their bleeding boy in and helping him? Was it true that God would kill their little girl because they came to the church to see us? Could we give them any help from the Bible to know what was right about this?

We quickly led them to the gospels and Jesus' claim that if you had seen him you had seen the Father, and we reminded them that Jesus came to show us what God was like. We told them to search and see if there was any instance of Jesus killing anyone, or putting sickness on anyone. We talked about the Good Samaritan and the way he helped the man who was beaten by thieves. They seemed to feel better.

Soon the evangelist was giving scripture also. The Good Samaritan was outside, not in, a church building. Also, in the Old Testament when David sinned, God took his baby.

Fear began to mount in all the people and they didn't know whom to believe. We prayed and asked God to help us know what to do, but we didn't hear any major breakthrough. We just had to ride out the storm.

Just when we felt we were recovering, it was announced that there would be a chapter house meeting. The subject—us! We hadn't been there long enough to really understand the consequences of this.

The chapter house was the local government, rather like a county seat, and meetings were held every Sunday. Most decisions were politically motivated, and every local happening was subject to discussion—everything from a farmer's grazing permit to disobedient teenagers to spouses in adultery could be brought before the chapter government. In this case, the same family who had complained to the denomination was at it again. (This family had a reputation locally for stealing from people and then testifying how the Lord had blessed them with their newfound possessions. Once while we were gone they had taken our big pots and pans; some of their relatives had seen them and returned them to us.)

Fortunately, we were oblivious to most of what was being said because it was in Navajo, but Tom and Millie translated the positive remarks and let us know who our friends were—and there were many, thank God! The meeting wore on and on and was adjourned without a decision that we knew of.

Time passed and little Tami remained very much alive, so some of the people got the message that possibly it was right to help Leroy in the church. They began to come back and listen a little more closely to what was being said.

Survival was becoming an issue, and it took all of us to keep everyone warm and fed. One day we drove out to the springs to fill our thirty-gallon container with water. When we got to the pipe with its usually overflowing trough, we found nothing but ice. Frozen! We'd have to drive fifteen miles to another spring. Saying a prayer that we'd have enough gas, we took Tom and Millie with us so they could

God Knows Where I Am

show us another location. It was also frozen. Undaunted by the looks of the situation, the guys took an axe and broke through the ice in the stock tank to get to the water.

By now it was late evening, and we started back up to Wheatfields. The roads were not so bad at the lower elevation, and we still had enough fuel. We had about five miles to go. It was getting dark and Don turned the lights on. I looked up just in time to see him hit the brakes hard—horses, running right in front of us! We barely missed the horses, and the whole thirty gallons of ice water flooded the Suburban and the boys in the back seat. Thank God, we had a heater, but the water was gone, and we'd have to make do somehow.

Should we leave? Or should we stay? Where would we go? Before we could make any decisions, we realized that one was being made for us. Snow blanketed the mountain day after day, getting deeper and making roads impassable. It began to be a real chore to keep our store of firewood, and then one day the unthinkable happened—the handle on our axe split completely in two. A temporary repair was made but it didn't hold up. No axe—and more snow coming.

It was early afternoon and a soft knock came at the door. It was Elizabeth, great brown eyes shining and face turned down. She was smiling and we knew she wanted something, but what? Perhaps she wanted to borrow our big stew pot? I offered it. She shook her head no. So we just asked, hoping she might understand more of our English than we did her Navajo. She said something that sounded like "adds" or "adz." Then she abruptly left and hurried down the path to her hogan.

Millie wasn't home, so Brian and Brett went down to the home of the Ben family to ask what "adz" was. They had several teens who spoke both English and Navajo. They could only think that it meant some kind of clothing.

After several hours Millie returned and went to see Elizabeth on our behalf. She came back laughing. Their father Chee had sent Elizabeth to get our axe head. He, who was nearly ninety years old, had hand-carved a solid oak handle for our axe and wanted to put it on. We were astonished! We did not even know he was aware that our axe handle was broken. We recognized that this was a survival blessing from God.

Blizzard conditions took over our little mountain home, and we tied a string from the church to the little outhouse up on the hill. Whenever anyone went outside, we watched carefully to make sure they got back in quickly. There was no way to go to the springs for water now—the stew pot was constantly being filled with snow to melt, and we conserved firewood as much as possible.

Two weeks passed, then three. There was no way to wash clothes and keep enough snow melted for drinking and cooking, so we wore our cleanest dirty socks and tried to make the best of it. Sometimes at night we would sit around the radio and see if we could get anything. We made fudge once or twice, read all the old magazines, committed the Readers Digest humor to memory, and really got to know each other. This was so different from our previous winters in Ohio when everyone went to his own room or watched television or visited friends and never talked to each other— now we shared our feelings about God and our dreams for the future. We spent time reworking math problems and talking about literature, comparing the Bible to authors of our day—we found the writings of God definitely superior. We even found things attributed to Shakespeare and Ben Franklin that came from the Bible.

Another two weeks passed, then another week. Our daily food was primarily fry bread and some beans, and then just bread. Finally, a Monday morning came with the stark realization that all we had was flour, some salt and a little baking powder—and of course, the ever present pot of melting snow. My pioneering spirit was exhausted. Complaining to the Lord became easy, although in the past I had been one of those who criticized the Hebrew children for complaining so much on their trek out of Egypt.

Fear began to rear its ugly head. All of the problems fought their way to the forefront of my thoughts, and in the middle of all that, I was upset most about one ridiculous thing—I didn't have any shortening. If I had lard, or old bacon grease, or something, I could make bread—but I didn't know how to keep it from sticking to the pan. Griping and complaining, I pleaded with the Lord to have mercy on us. Brian, Brett, and Brad went to all the neighboring homes asking if anyone had anything we could borrow—but they had all been snowed in for six weeks as well—no one else had anything either.

Laughing, Brian said, "They're all having snow soup too."

Suddenly in tears, I said, *Lord, even the widow in the Bible had flour and oil!* Remembering the story of the woman who had gotten down to her last flour and a little oil, I questioned God.

Outside, it was bright daylight. There was even a little sunshine inside, reflected from the deep snow and the frozen Suburban that had remained parked in one spot for so long. No one was in the building but me—and I heard a voice. I do not know if it was spoken aloud, or just registered inside me, but it was very clear. *"You have oil."*

Startled I looked up at the little pulpit in the building that was now church, home, and survival for us. There was a tiny bottle of anointing oil.

Catching my breath at the thought of it, I said, *Lord, I can't use that!*

Just as quickly the voice came, *"Yes, you can. David used the shewbread."* (see 1 Samuel 21:6)

Soon we gathered as a family asking God to bless the most anointed bread we had ever eaten!

The boys left after the meal and went to visit the teenagers who lived nearby. Someone had managed to get through to their home with food that day, and sandwiches were offered to them. Somehow they didn't feel they could accept when Dad, Mom, and little Reesie (their sister Larissa) weren't with them.

As they started out the door to go home, Jim, the father of their friends, touched Brian on the shoulder. He did not speak English, but he had heard our boys address each other with the word, "Hey!" So he said "Hey!"

As Brian turned around, he put a bag of groceries in his hand and waved him on. The boys ran across the icy hill to get to the church. In the bag, we found hamburger, a box of Hamburger Helper, a loaf of bread and a six-pack of their favorite soft drink, Mountain Dew. It was a feast! Once again, God had shown us that he knew where we were and had made a way.

CHAPTER 9

A Narrow Road Rising Up

In February, we were able to get out one day and run a few errands. We decided to visit our friends in Waterflow, New Mexico, and spend the night there. When we came back to Wheatfields the next day and turned onto our road, snow once again barred the way. The Ben family had been trying for seven hours to get their truck out to the highway, and now they turned their attention to getting us back in. The procedure was simple—don't get frustrated and don't hurry—push, shove, drive a few feet, and if it sinks too far, jack it up—then lean against the Suburban and push it off the jack so it gets out of the rut. Try again. If it's dark, you build a fire to keep warming your hands. Don't put the fire out; leave it for the next truck trying to get in—it's very wet, and there's nothing nearby but snow, so it won't burn anything. When you get a hundred feet or so, build another fire and keep working.

It took almost another seven hours.

After a few days, it was possible at times to get in and out, and we had a request for prayer for Jim Ben, our close neighbor. He was in the Indian Hospital in Gallup, about seventy miles away. Tom and Millie needed to go to Gallup and see if they could sell their cradleboards, so they bought the gas and we went to see Jim.

Jim decided he had had enough of hospital life, and when he looked out the hospital window and saw the Suburban, he signed himself out. He met us at the elevator and made it clear he was going home with us. Who could argue? He didn't speak English.

Tom bought some hot dogs and bread for us to take home and soon we were turning onto the icy dirt road—and that was all we did—we couldn't get any further. We would have to walk in. Then someone suggested we just wait until the slushy mud froze a little and then try driving.

"Mom, I don't want to wait. I'm hungry." Larissa's little voice from the back seat reminded me that my stomach was rumbling, too. Out came the hot dogs, a fire was built, and right there on the side of the highway we had a wiener roast. However, we had a small problem—no sticks or coat hangers were available.

"I can fix that." In seconds, Brian had liberated the curtain rods from the back of the Suburban and turned them into hot dog roasters. Soon there were other cars stopping to see what the occasion was. People continued to join us as Brian, Brett, and Brad entertained them with their imitations of well-known comedians. The time passed quickly, and soon we drove in on frozen ground.

The snow and ice lingered a while longer, but we were seeing some sunshine during the day now. It was even possible to go outside without a coat. We longed for a hot shower and the wonderful smell of freshly laundered clothes. For three months our total income had been only a few dollars. Every time the boys went out to get wood, they put plastic bread bags over their socks to try and keep their feet dry. Sometimes it worked.

The roads were beginning to melt, but now there were different problems. The spring muds came flooding down the hillsides into the roads, and falling into it was like dropping into a vat of chocolate pudding. The cars still weren't going anywhere.

Some of the people had left the mountain and gone to spend the winter with relatives at a lower elevation, but those who stayed kept fighting the little road to get in and out. Tom got together with Don, Brian, Brett, and Brad, and they began to carve out a path higher on the side of the hill. The melting slush had no place to go once it got to the road, and nothing changed until it dried. So they built one section of road higher up, fortifying it with rocks and logs and whatever they could find.

Wednesday night came and only a few people showed up for church. There was no gas for the generator and no fuel for the lanterns. Maybe we should just cancel the service.

The door opened wide and someone turned his car lights on to shine through the door, making just enough light for Bible reading. It was a good service. People lingered in the dark to talk.

With slightly warmer nights, we could sometimes sleep on the bus again if we used enough blankets. We fell asleep, feeling warm and blessed to be together, but still wondering what God was doing with us.

The sun was just coming up when Brett got up and stepped outside. He couldn't believe what he saw. Lying there on the ground, all crumpled up, was twenty dollars! He ran back in to tell us, and we all wondered if this was a blessing from the Lord for us. But as we talked it over, we knew that someone had lost that money, and Brett wanted to find out who. So he immediately went to Tom and Millie's house to ask if they had heard of anyone losing money. As he came to their door, he could smell the coffee and he heard Tom saying, "I know I had it in my pocket."

"What are you looking for?" Brett asked.

"My money to go to the laundromat. We got up early to go wash, and now we can't find what we did with the money."

"How much was it?"

"Twenty dollars."

"Well, you shouldn't throw your money on the ground," Brett laughed. "Here it is."

And he related to them his early morning find. Probably when Tom took his car keys out of his pocket the money had fallen out.

To Tom, this was a startling event. He related the story to a friend, and quickly everyone was talking about the white boy who looked for the real owner of the money he found—and the thing that made it astonishing was that everyone knew how much use he or his family could have made of that twenty dollars!

Sunshine coming into the bus made a very comfortable setting in the afternoons, and sometimes Tom and Millie would come and just talk, or ask questions about the Bible. One late winter afternoon, they questioned us, "How did you come to be here?"

We began the long story of the Wednesday night missionary service in our church when the guest speaker began talking about the Native Americans, and how our hearts were stirred at his words. We talked about our first and second summer tours of the Reservations in Oklahoma, New Mexico, and Arizona, and the astonishing things that happened as we traveled with twenty-seven people. The first year we had a blown engine in our van when we got into Oklahoma, making the rest of the trip impossible to complete. But God sent a complete stranger to loan us his vehicle to finish the trip.

We tried to make the story short, but eventually we told them about the request God had made of us: *"Who will go, and whom shall I send?"* (Isaiah 6:8, author paraphrase)

Quitting jobs and giving away all but basic necessities, we had left with no money or certainty except the Word of God.

When we finished, Millie began her own story. She was one of several children born to Chee and Anna Etcitty. Her mother was a medicine woman. Most of the people on their mountaintop had problems with alcohol. The little stream running down the mountain was called Whiskey Creek. Her mother died and her father Chee grew older, seeing many of his loved ones die. Millie had two little boys and a little girl, and she also drank. Her children began to grow up and she met Tom Begay, a Marine who was half Navajo and half Hopi. Tom also had a penchant for alcohol, and could become violent when drinking. They moved into a hogan and had a little girl they named Tami.

A preacher started coming to visit them and tried to tell them about Jesus, but Tom just didn't want to talk to him. Still he continued to come. One day Tom looked out his window and saw the familiar figure coming. He knew the preacher had to go around a curve before reaching their hogan, so he hurriedly ran outside and put a large padlock on his front door. Then rushing to the back, he climbed in the window and told his wife to be very quiet. When the preacher saw the lock, he would think they were gone and would go away. In a few minutes, the preacher reached the front of the house and knocked on the door. Little Tami, just learning to talk, called out, "Come in."

"I know you're in there, Tom. Whenever you're ready to talk, let me know."

Tom couldn't resist determination like that. He listened and made a decision to give his heart to the Lord.

In the meantime, Millie's father Chee became very ill. They took him to the Indian Hospital in Gallup, and his condition worsened. At his age, everyone knew it was just a matter of time. He lapsed into a coma—and then he had a dream, or a vision, or something. He saw a very wide road going down into blackness. There were many people on that road, and they seemed to be on fire, or their clothes were on fire. The wailing and moaning was terrible, and he soon realized that he was one of them. He couldn't even describe the depth of the evil he felt. Looking backward he saw another road, a narrow one rising up. There was a person—a presence—someone—on that other road. It was so beautiful and filled with light—how he wished he were on that other road! As soon as he began to think about it, the beautiful presence spoke to him.

"Chee, you've been leading people down that dark road all your life. You can be on this road if you want to, but you must go back and tell them that Jesus really is God."

At that, Chee woke up and there was a man standing by his bed who was a Christian. The man prayed a prayer of repentance with him and Chee was saved. Then he got better and went home to Wheatfields mountain. Calling all his family together, he told them that they were going to have a church. They dammed up Whiskey Creek, changed the name to Jordan River, and kind of baptized each other. They designated a little house to be their church. Of course, they needed a pastor, so they called on the newly saved Tom Begay to fill that position. Tom said he would do the best he could, but he didn't know anything about the Bible. So they began to pray that the Lord would send somebody to teach them.

Then one day they heard a missionary team speak, and they invited them to come and hold a week of services. Not preaching—they just wanted to ask questions and have things explained every night. The missionary team came, and a few miles before they arrived, their bus broke down. Tom and Millie found the bus on the highway and towed it up to be parked beside the church. That big blue school bus was the one we were sitting in as Millie related the story. We were their answer to prayer

Towing the blue bus to Wheatfields

The blue bus, Suburban, and Wheatfields Church

CHAPTER 10

Big Texas Style Toast

It was the middle of March. Winter still clutched us in its icy fingers, threatening one storm after another and prompting wishes for the sight of blossoming trees and dry ground—maybe even sunburn. The books had all been read, the Reader's Digest stories thoroughly discussed, and the humor put to memory. Wood chopping muscles were finely tuned. Beans and fry bread filled stomachs, but totally without glamour.

"Can you take us to Gallup if we buy you gas?" It was very early in the morning. Framed by the door in the last of the moonlight, Tom and Millie stood asking the question, not looking at all as sleepy as we felt. "We have to go now, while the ground is frozen. If we wait till the sun gets warm, the car will sink in the mud."

Absolutely right!

Twenty minutes and eighteen layers of clothing later we were on our way. We knew from experience that we might be walking back from the highway in heavy snow, and we'd better be prepared. Without a penny in our pockets, and no ready-made food to take with us for the children when they got hungry, once again we reminded the Lord that we belonged to him. The winter had been long and hard. We had not received any money other than some change for two months, and we felt totally cut off from the rest of the world. There had been no letters from home, no little "Thinking of You" cards, no reminders that anyone knew we still existed. It was seventy miles to the post office, and we had driven there many times to find an empty mailbox.

Soon the familiar streets of Gallup and the brick post office building were in sight. I held my breath as Don went into the post office and came back out with some envelopes. I opened one—a note to say, "We are praying for you."

Thank God somebody is. We need it.

Another of the same, from people we didn't know that well. With a sigh of relief, I watched a five-dollar bill fall from the next card.

Thank you, Jesus! That will buy bread and bologna at Safeway for the children. They won't have to go long without food.

I felt the car easing into traffic as I read the short letters and wondered what had prompted them. They were not from family or people we had known a long time. Some of the names were new to us. Don was already on the way to chauffeur Tom and Millie to take care of their business, and I was anxious to get to the store and get sandwiches made. The thought of bologna sandwiches made me feel so good—in fact, it was mouth-watering! I wondered if I could even explain that feeling to anyone who had never been really hungry.

Opening the last envelope, I found a check from a church in Ohio, and a letter. The letter said that the church was having a special missionary emphasis that week and they had chosen us to write letters to. Enclosed was their check in the amount of one hundred dollars! I nearly fell off the seat—no one could possibly know what a fortune one hundred dollars was to us at that time! We could buy groceries and—praise the Lord—I could do laundry! Real clean clothes—I wouldn't have to melt snow until I got a bucket of water, choose the most needed items to rub on rough, dry, chapped hands, and then try to find a place to hang them where they wouldn't freeze or drip on anything—we could go to the laundromat—*Hallelujah!*

Mentally I calculated the cost, subtracting the tithe, the gas to get to town, and the cost of detergent. We could do everything and have twenty or twenty-five dollars left over if I was careful buying groceries. Oh, yes, I would need stamps to answer the letters.

What a blessing!

I wondered, *would it be all right? No, I couldn't—it would be too much of a luxury. It was enough to have the urgent needs met. Still...*

"Mommy, I'm hungry."

"Yeah, Mom, we haven't had breakfast." Brad's voice was beginning to get deeper and he sounded almost like Brian.

A chorus of "me too!" came from the back.

I prayed silently, *Lord, would it be okay? They've never complained.*

"Honey, how about that special at the truck stop?" Don suggested exactly what I was thinking. "The French toast is 'all you can eat for $1.99,' and that would really fill these kids up."

"And bankrupt the restaurant, probably," Brian laughed. "I could eat a horse."

"I'd rather have the French toast," Brett grinned. "Not as tough as horse."

So it was settled.

The Union 76 sign loomed big ahead of us now. The check had been cashed. $1.99 each for nine people would be about eighteen dollars, plus drinks and tax.

"Table for nine, please."

"Yes ma'am. Nine orders of French toast? I s'pose these boys will want a second order—it's all you can eat, same price, y'know. Big Texas style toast."

I loved the drawl. Red hair flying and big eyes sparkling, the waitress couldn't have seen her twentieth birthday yet.

"Yes, ma'am."

"All righty, I'll just go ahead and have the second plates cooked up. What d'y'all want ta drank, five cawfees? One white milk? Oh, no, three white milks? And you, honey, what do you wont? What was that? Root beer? Did he say *root beer?*"

"Brad, are you sure you want root beer with syrupy French toast?"

"He wants root beer. Give him root beer."

Nine heads bowed and a looong prayer commenced. The waitress came with huge plates of steaming French toast laced with butter and sprinkled with powdered sugar. She put the coffee pot on the table and waited patiently as the prayer continued. The boys didn't look up—the grins on their faces were evidence that they were not only grateful, but they knew the anticipation was half the joy of the meal. I confess I watched.

"Amen!" chorused nine voices.

"Here's yer milk, and one root beer. Y'all enjoy yer meal."

I don't think they ever had so many reorders on that breakfast special—but on this freezing day in March, the blessing was doubly appreciated.

We decided not to buy many groceries, just a few, and the next day we'd shop for food and do the laundry—slowly, so we could enjoy it!

When Tom and Millie finished the things they had to do in Gallup the sun was going down, and we drove back to the mountain. We waited until we were sure the road had frozen, and then Don turned our faithful GMC Suburban onto the path that sufficed for a road.

The next day was cold and windy, and signs of snow were in the air. Still rejoicing in what we knew was God's provision, we sorted laundry, chopped wood, and answered letters. Cooking and cleaning up was a formidable task—it took a long time to build fires, melt snow for dishwater, heat the water, and then wash the dishes and the gruesome, blackened pots and pans. How nice it had been yesterday to get up from the table and leave the clean-up for someone else.

It was mid-afternoon before all the chores were done and we were ready for the forty-mile round trip to Navajo, the small crossroads town where the laundromat was. Funny, I couldn't remember looking forward to going to the laundromat before—I had always looked on it as a real pain, and even dreaded it. But today I was actually excited and anxious to get there, imagining the smell of fresh, clean laundry and the happy absence of dirty socks!

CHAPTER 11

Under the Shadow of the Almighty

I noticed Don checking the heavy clouds coming in over the mountain, and I knew what he was thinking. We had enough gas to get there and a little more, but we'd have to buy gas at the little station in Navajo before we came home. If it snowed while we were gone, we'd have to leave our clean clothes in the car and walk a mile and a half up the mountain to get home. We had already gone several miles, past the lake and the mountain we called Sleeping Chief—if we turned back now, we might not have enough gas to make the trip again later.

Within minutes, the snow was coming in soft flurries. I usually kept a thermos in the back with hot coffee, and I busied myself pouring a cup for Don. Offering it to him just as we hit a slippery spot on the road, I held on until the Suburban was rolling instead of sliding. The windshield wipers began to struggle as the wet snow clung to them and we began to think about what the results might be. Remembering the comforting words of Psalm 91 was a help to my mind. *"He is my refuge and my fortress: my God; in him will I trust."* (Psalm 91:2)

Other vehicles had pulled off the road and stopped. By the time the little settlement of Navajo came into view, the flurries had changed to fiercely driven snow—blizzard conditions! We had learned to keep blankets and water in the car (Brian, Brett, and Brad were always correcting me—I called it a car; they insisted it was a truck.) We stopped to buy gasoline.

There were no lights on at the service station—there was no gas available. The storm had knocked out all the electricity in Navajo, including the laundromat. We couldn't go back to Wheatfields without buying gas, and there was a distinct possibility that we did not have enough fuel even to get to the next town. What if we ran out before we got there, or got stuck in snow on the way?

I could see furrows above Don's eyebrows. He didn't say anything—he wouldn't—he didn't have to. Brian was keeping up a light and easy chatter. He understood also, but he didn't want anyone to worry. Even if we made it to the next town without running out of gas, we'd still have to drive up the mountain roads in the blizzard to get home, and even if we made it up the highway, there was still a mile and a half to walk in the dark, carrying little Larissa in blinding snow. If it was this bad here, it would be worse on the mountain.

When we lived in Ohio, things were different in winter storms or if our car broke down. We'd just walk to the nearest house and borrow a telephone, and there were several people we could call to come and help us—my family, Don's family, neighbors, church friends, people Don worked with—but here? Even if there was a house, most of these people didn't have telephones. And they might not speak English. And they might not like white people. And there was no one to call.

The wheels were spinning in the ice and snow, and the chatter stopped. I was glad we all knew how to pray. This trip had never seemed so long before.

As we whispered "Praise the Lord," the lights of Window Rock became barely visible. We pulled into the gas station and the boys pumped the gas. Don pondered the situation. Our last midnight walk up the mountain had been life threatening. It would not be wise to try that tonight. We had about thirty-five dollars after buying gas. If we limited the laundry to ten dollars, and if we could get a motel room for twenty dollars, we could drive into Gallup, spend the night, and go back up on the mountain in the daytime. We would have to try. More prayer.

God, couldn't you make this a little bit easier?

I hoped I had just been thinking, and not speaking my thoughts aloud.

And what if we can't get a room for twenty dollars?

Don't plan for failure.

Lord, it seems I'm holding my breath a lot lately. Does that mean I don't really trust you to take care of us? I'm trying not to do that, Lord.

Okay, I think I'm together now. Walk boldly up to the desk, just like you've got plenty of money. One of us can ask the clerk how much for a room for one night. It would be cheaper for just two people, but Christians don't lie. Yes, four children, two adults.

"This is quite a night for weather, isn't it? I'm glad I don't have to be out in it. Are you folks traveling far from home?" the clerk at the desk asked.

"No," I answered. "We live about seventy miles from here."

"Oh, really? What do you do out there? Are you teaching school?"

"We're missionaries on the Navajo Reservation." Don answered, reaching for Larissa's hand. Her eyes were open wide, taking in all the glitter and candies and toys.

"Well, I thought I recognized you. Aren't you the ones who came to our church about two years back? Well, we're not supposed to do this, but let me check with the manager." In a few minutes, she was back. "He said to just charge you for two people. That'll be twenty dollars, please. Room 206."

The breath escaped. *Sorry about that, Lord. Keep working on me.*

It took a few minutes to tear everyone away from the shiny boots and jewelry and candies of the store, and the wonderful smells of the truck stop restaurant. We found the number on the door, and Don did his usual, "Boys, be quiet and don't disturb people in the other rooms."

An honest to goodness hot shower—clean children—squeaky clean hair—and television—we haven't seen television in four months!

"Hey, Mom! Civilization. Guess what? You turn this little shiny thing and water comes out!"

"Hey, no icicles on the seat!"

"I miss the spider webs in the outhouse."

"Wow, look at this—you flip this switch and it gets light!" On...off...on...off...on...

"All right, you guys, enough clowning."

Even Don's gruff command to settle down didn't have much of the usual fatherly bark. They were having fun and we were glad to see it. I think we all got wrinkled skin from being in the water too long. All those months of sponge baths, getting up early and building fires, struggling with wicks on lanterns, carrying and heating water, melting snow, and scrubbing black pots and pans gave us a real appreciation for convenience.

It wasn't long before we all fell asleep, with no idea what was in store for us the next morning.

Chapter 12

Do We Have to Do It This Way?

Morning? Already morning?
I had cereal in the car, and enough milk for breakfast. It was almost frozen, but it thawed quickly in the warm motel room. We took one last look to make sure we had not left anything and returned the key to the desk.

The laundromat was busy, and we waited to get change from the attendant. Larissa found a candy machine and looked longingly at it, but we had to make every quarter count. We had sorted the "absolutely must have's" from the "this can wait" items; now we washed and dried them. I had enough laundry money for one more wash but not for the dryer, so some of the towels would have to be spread out to dry by the fire at home. By the time we were finished, it was late afternoon and bitter cold outside. I wrapped a clean blanket around Larissa and hurried to the Suburban. One last check of the mailbox at the Gallup post office, and it was empty. We still had plenty of daylight to get home in, and the snow had stopped.

Now a new expression on Don's face caused me to ask, "What?"

"I smell gas."

"Maybe it's the Coleman lantern. I brought it with us."

"No, that's not it."

"The car sounds funny."

"It doesn't sound funny, Mom. It sounds bad; there's a difference between funny and bad!" Every now and then I regretted trying to teach my sons correct usage of the English language—no, it wasn't "funny."

Don said, "Honey, there's gas pouring out—we've got a broken fuel line. Do you have change? We have to buy a clamp."

It was getting very cold, and we couldn't leave the Suburban running. Soon the clamp was on, but Don still had the hood up. It was leaking somewhere else. Pulling blankets out of the laundry, we tried to find a way to keep warm. Snow was falling again and it was getting dark. I decided to light the Coleman lantern to see if it would knock off the chill in the car—but would it be safe with the windows closed?

Gallup. Not the safest place to be at night. No money. Bitter cold. Lord, I'm holding my breath again. Once again—pray first—analyze the situation—look for an answer.

I looked down at my wrist. I was wearing a bracelet given to me by a friend. When the Navajos had an emergency, they went to a pawnshop. Could I do that? I'd never been in a pawnshop in my life.

Trying to think the situation through, I asked the Lord to show me if there was something I needed to understand. Vaguely I recalled some prayer I had prayed, asking the Lord to help us understand what the Navajo people were feeling and going through. *Did I really pray that?*

The closest pawnshop was still open. Most were closed. There was a man at the desk polishing something. I wasn't sure what to do, so I held up the bracelet.

"How much for my bracelet?"
"You want it back?"
"Of course."
"How much do you want?"
"I need at least twenty-five dollars," I told him quietly. "You see, I have this emergency..."
"Everybody has emergencies. Ten dollars for the bracelet."
"But it's worth..."
"Ten dollars," he said as he reached for the closed sign to put on the door.
"Oh."
"Got anything else?" The man was looking at my watch. I held it up and he reached out to take it.
"Twenty dollars for both. Pay twenty-two dollars in thirty days and you get 'em back."

My face was stinging, red. *The nerve of that man—twenty dollars!* I went back to the car on the street and showed Don what I had done, then asked, "Can you make it back to that same motel? We can walk over to that little store and get bologna and bread with our change."

"Do I have a choice?" Don asked.

No one was complaining, but I knew nerves were a little tight. We walked slowly up to the desk at the motel. It was a different clerk.

"Could we get the same room we had last night?"
"Which room?" she asked.
"206. And could we get it at the same price?"
"What price?"
"Twenty dollars."
"Are you sure? We don't have any rooms for that price."
"I have my receipt."
"Oh, ok, twenty dollars."

I breathed. *I don't like this, Lord. It's so embarrassing. Do we have to do it this way? I know I prayed for under-*

standing, but couldn't you give it to me some other way? Oh, well—one thing at a time—at least we can relax for another night. Tomorrow morning I'm sure you'll show Don how to fix the car and everything will be great. Maybe there will even be money in the mail.

The next morning we arose with high hopes. I'm not sure there was any faith there—just hope. It was Saturday, and the post office would close at noon. We stayed until checkout time, giving the post office plenty of time to get all the mail up before we drove over there.

It was March 20. The next day was Sunday—and Brad's birthday. He would be twelve. It seemed we were in a different world now from past birthdays when we had gone shopping and baked a cake and planned a party. Empty mailbox, possibly a bad fuel pump—was there anything else we could pawn? Yes, our 35mm camera. Don took it in. They wouldn't take cameras. We tried another pawnshop. They reluctantly said yes. It was our very last resource—but it provided enough to buy food and a fuel pump.

The gas had stopped leaking and the Suburban was running...

Now what? Three blocks from the post office, it just quit. Don started it again—it quit again. It would start, but it wouldn't run.

That feeling began to creep up on me—all over—just a feeling of, *I want to go to sleep. Just let me go to sleep, and I'll wake up, and this will just be a bad dream.*

You can't go to sleep when you have four children, and it's very cold, and you know it's getting dark, and your husband has been strong as long as he can.

What next? Has God really abandoned us? Were the people right, who told us we were crazy to believe that God would send us to minister to the Navajos? Have we missed God somewhere?

Thoughts crowded into my mind that I wouldn't allow there before. *What if God hasn't really called us? Maybe we were just lucky before.* I couldn't even remember anything God had done for us.

I began to force my mind to hold on to the Bible verses that meant something to me. My head felt like it was in a vise.

How could God do this to us? Didn't he say he would supply all our needs? Of course, we weren't his big guns; we were just little people in the battle. I guess maybe we don't count. Are we expendable?

Tired. Just plain tired. Too cold to fall asleep.

"Mom?"

No—Brett, please don't ask me anything. I don't know anything. The words were not spoken aloud, just in my mind, so he didn't hear them.

"Mom, it's Saturday night."

Chapter 13

Did I Really Pray That?

"We're always saying that we'd like to be in Gallup on Saturday night so we can check out the Christian Coffee House—we're only a block and a half away." Brian's comment completed Brett's question.

"Better than sitting here in the cold," Brad added.

"Are you going, Don?" I asked. I didn't really want to go, but I didn't want the boys on the street alone in Gallup on a Saturday night. We had talked a lot about going to see what this place was like. We had operated a Christian Coffee House in Ohio for several years, and I knew our boys missed it.

"Yes, I guess I will."

"Well, Larissa and I will wait here for you."

"Lock the doors, Mom. Are you sure you aren't going?" Brian was in a hurry; Brett and Brad were already racing down the street.

As they were leaving I reached into the laundry basket and pulled out clean blankets for Larissa and me, glad that I had brought blankets to wash. We still had some cold cuts and bread, but I couldn't make myself think beyond the next hour. There were few lights here, and the dark of the winter evening was already blanketing the city. Cold winds whistled around us, and I tried to get Larissa to snuggle into the blanket.

"Mommy, I want to go."

"Reesie, be still and get under this blanket; it's cold!" She tried to sit still, but finally I knew it wouldn't work.

"Mommy, I have to go to the bathroom."

I looked down the street, hoping to find some place with restrooms that wouldn't be very far to walk. I buttoned her coat and locked the door, and then we started walking reluctantly in the direction Don and her brothers had gone. Maybe they would have a bathroom there.

Actually, I was walking reluctantly. Larissa was tugging at my hand and almost running. I knew that I'd have to keep my mind clear or I'd have tears frozen to my face when I got there, and I didn't want anyone to ask any questions.

Long before we reached the storefront, I could hear and feel the booming bass drum and guitar, and Larissa just ran faster. She was up the steps and rushing to get inside. Warm air blew into my face, and it felt good.

What do I have on? Am I dressed appropriately for this? Or does it matter?

The band on stage was belting out a gospel version of a popular country song. They had changed the words of "Elvira" and were singing about "Hellfire." Moving easily from that into a soft invitation, they had everyone's attention. Young people were seated everywhere—on the floor, on chairs, and on the sides of the stage. I watched as they approached my sons. Young men and young women asked them, "Do you know Jesus as your Savior and Lord?" And over and over the answer came back, "Yes, I do!" Something stirred inside me every time I heard them affirm their salvation.

"Welcome, brother!"

Well, at least, Lord, you've provided a diversion for them for a little while. But it's getting colder and later outside, and soon we'll have to go back to the car and face facts.

A young man with a strong Spanish accent approached me and asked, "Hey, are you these guys' mom?"

"Yes, I am."

"Are you saved?"

"Yes, I am."

Usually this kind of question would start a conversation that I really enjoyed, but this time I had nothing more to say.

The same young man was now asking Brad, "Hey, can you come to our church in the morning? We've got a great church! Where do you live?"

"We're from Wheatfields, Arizona. We're missionaries to the Navajos." Brad sounded very confident.

"Are you going back tonight? Maybe you could stay over and come to church?" Now another young man was asking questions.

"Well, we're not sure yet," Brett sidestepped the question.

"Do you have a place to stay?"

"Not exactly. Actually, we broke down and we've got to get our Suburban fixed," Brian finally told him.

I slipped into the back of the room, looking for the restroom and waiting for them to get ready to leave. When I came back out, Don was looking for me.

"Danny says their church has a home for transients here, and we could probably sleep there tonight. We could sleep on the floor in the living room; at least it would be warm. I'm going to go with him to talk to the Pastor and see if it's okay, so stay here till I get back," Don said.

He seemed to be taking it all in stride, as though this were a very normal situation. He had no idea that I felt as though my world had caved in and God had let me down and I didn't know where to go from here or how to resurrect my faith.

It seemed a long time before Don came back. He had a puzzled look on his face. I was so tired that even the transient home didn't seem such a bad idea, especially with a four-year-old who was already way past her bedtime.

"Well, what did he say?"

"He said, 'Absolutely not.' We're going back to the car."

Don didn't offer any more information.

Why should I be surprised? Par for the course, I guess. Even though I felt betrayed and exhausted, deep down inside I could feel something saying, *"Pay attention. You need to remember this. Keep every detail in your memory."*

My mind wandered back to last year's March. We were just getting ready to leave Ohio at this time a year ago. What had been accomplished since then? We had no real home, no income, and had barely made a few Navajo friends. Would it always be this way? How long could we keep going like this? Were all those things we called answered prayers just coincidence?

Later I would discover that this was Satan's tool, placing thoughts against God in our minds and waiting for us to act on them. When the Bible speaks of "casting down imaginations" and "bringing every thought into the captivity of Christ," this is what it means—but for now, I just let those thoughts ramble wildly through my mind, thinking they were my own reasoning.

My conclusion was that either we had seriously missed God, or God had let us down.

CHAPTER 14

In His Hands
THE ROYAL SUITE

"Danny's going to tow the Suburban somewhere. Just get Reesie and come on." Don was already following Danny out the door, and I hurried to keep up with him and the boys. We climbed into the Suburban and pulled blankets around us, shivering in the cold. I kept asking where we were going, but he didn't know. In a few minutes, the truck turned into a parking lot and stopped. The young man told us to come with him, and we dutifully followed.

He led us through the lobby of a motel and upstairs, opening a door with a brass label on it that said THE ROYAL SUITE. Before we had a chance to sink into the carpet or explore the rooms, he began to explain.

"We have a very unusual church. Most of our people are Anglo, with some Hispanic and some Navajo. But our Pastor is Navajo. I told him that you were staying way out there on the mountain ministering to the Navajos and your car broke down. I asked him if you could stay at the transient house, and he said, 'Absolutely not! No way! These are

God's messengers to my people, and we will give them the best we've got to offer! Assign an escort to them for church tomorrow. Take them out to breakfast and dinner, and see that the car gets fixed. Find the best facility in town and see that everything they need is supplied.'"

The thoughts I had about God letting us down suddenly changed to, *This is the good news. What's the bad news?*

My spirit began to identify that painful voice. I didn't have enough strength to shut it down yet, but at least it was beginning to be recognizable.

The suite was beautiful—separate rooms and kitchen facilities, king size beds, toiletries far beyond the usual bar of soap, different television sets and many channels to choose from. Once again I was glad we had been to the laundromat. We had clean clothes available for Sunday morning church, and there was even an iron in the room.

By that time, I had decided to enjoy what was happening and think it through later. We assured Danny that we would be available when the church van came for us at seven-thirty the next morning—they were taking us out to breakfast, and then to their church. After church, they would take us to lunch, stop at a grocery store so we could buy sandwich supplies in case anyone got hungry later, and then bring us back to the motel. They would come back to pick us up for the evening service, and then return us to the motel for a second night. Monday they would get parts for the Suburban, and we could be on our way home.

When the alarm rang Sunday morning, my eyes opened slowly as I felt the warmth of the room. We weren't accustomed to waking up in a warm room—normally the fire had to be built first. That was my first thought. The second thought was *It's March 21!*

"Hey, Mom." The boys were already climbing out of bed, ready for whatever adventure the day held. I didn't want to get up yet.

"Mom, I was hoping there would be something special for my birthday. But don't you think God went a little overboard?"

Brad—he's 12 years old today! I had asked God to help us do something special for his birthday!

Inside I could sense that gentle voice saying, *"Yes. But much more than that—pay attention."*

The day was wonderful. There was even a chocolate cake. It was so different to be in a service where we were ministered to, and where we could sing and praise God without thinking about anything else. We rejoiced together and talked about all the things we could think of that God had done for us. Now there were many, unlike the night before when all was darkness and gloom.

When the day was over, I couldn't fall asleep. Every little detail of the last few weeks seemed to play itself through my mind. I couldn't comprehend just what was happening. So much apparent lack, and yet today so much blessing. Why?

That gentle voice, speaking without words, showed me a picture of myself. Every time provisions came I stretched them as far as I could. Every dollar was treated as though it would be the last one we'd receive. No luxuries could be allowed, because there might not be any more for a while. My flawed thinking had been operating in fear, not in faith. Yes, I had trusted God, but not in the way he wanted me to. If he had sent money to me then, I would have stretched it out to last for weeks. We would never have gone to a luxury hotel, or gone out to a restaurant twice in one day.

Then I knew what had happened. God had to take the whole situation out of our hands in order to bless us. He was helping us put it all back in his hands for the journey ahead...

Epilogue

It is amazing to look back on your life and see the daily living translated into annual collections of events. Having read many authors' biographies, I look over mine and wonder how time could have passed so quickly!

I was born into a huge, wonderful family in the southernmost part of West Virginia. My Dad, a coal miner, went to be with Jesus when I was sixteen, and we moved to Ohio. In the years following, Don Cartwright came into my life and blessed me with Brian, Brett, Brad and Larissa.

We had a strong call from God to begin ministry to the unchurched and street people. In 1973, we opened Operation Praise The Lord, a Christian Coffee House, and also began a prison ministry. In 1979, an invitation came to tour several American Indian Reservations. Repeating that tour in 1980, we knew that God had called us to the southwest USA to stay.

In order to obey that call, my husband Don had to leave his job, and we had no other source of income for our family of six. We struggled and prayed for months. Finally the courage came for us and two other families to give up all we had and start across the country with our children. We made it to Oklahoma before we ran out of money. God revealed Himself to us over and over as we prayed daily for His will.

We rented a mailbox in Gallup, NM, and there were very few letters coming to that address. Every day we prayed for direction, and every day something happened. Eventually we spent three months touring the Navajo Indian Reservation, and we were invited to go to Wheatfields, Arizona, for a week of meetings. Our bus broke down fourteen miles before we arrived on the Wheatfields mountain in 1981.

The bus is still on the mountain. The little frame building they used for a church has been replaced by two new buildings, and those buildings were recently joined together.

After almost two years, we moved into New Mexico. We were exhausted and urgently in need of a mission building to work from. We also needed to find a way to raise support for our family. We had no idea that the New Mexico move was part of God's plan for the next assignment. Hundreds of alcoholics congregated in the Waterflow, New Mexico area and many were getting killed on the highway. Almost every week the sirens blared, and at night twenty-five or thirty men, sometimes women, would knock on our door and ask for food, blankets, transportation, prayer, or something else. Some slept in our car, others on the ground. Our family had a tiny apartment, and we could let some of the women sleep on the floor.

In 1985, God made it possible for us to buy the old Sacred Heart Academy building from a very nice family who had lived there for several years. It had over fifty rooms, and soon we were detoxing and praying with many people in urgent need every day. They came from across the Navajo Nation and other Reservations. Some miraculous events brought many to know Jesus. Three bars operating near us kept emergency services constantly busy, just as we were.

Today all three bars are closed. The number of street people in Waterflow is small. Across the Navajo Nation there are still large numbers of addicted people, but we are praying for mighty moves of God.

The Navajo Nation is a huge area, as large as the state of West Virginia. Mission teams are now coming to Many Waters every summer, and churches are being built, repaired, and encouraged. Teams built a warehouse for us, and we've been able to help thousands of needy families.

Lynn Cartwright
Waterflow, New Mexico
April 2006

Many Waters Mission Today

As Lynn indicated in her epilogue, the Cartwrights continued living on the mountain in the blue school bus for almost two years, and then moved to the rural community of Waterflow, New Mexico, about half a mile from the Navajo Reservation border, where they continue as missionaries to the Navajos, and operate Many Waters Mission. The four children are grown, the three boys have married, and all four children continue to help with the work of the Mission. Others help also, donating time, finances, materials, and prayer. The Mission supplies food for the hungry as well as clothing, blankets, building materials, Bibles, and training in the Word of God—overseeing or helping more than twenty churches scattered thinly across the vastness of the Navajo Reservation. Youth groups and church work teams come to help—building and repairing church buildings and homes, conducting Vacation Bible Schools, holding open air services, and sending special gifts and food that bless many families at Thanksgiving and Christmas. A large warehouse has been built with donated materials and labor to shelter items until they are distributed. Included on the mission site are dorms, showers, and kitchen facilities for the visiting youth and work teams, a chapel, a library, and the warehouse. *Christian Relief Services*, *Feed the Children*, and *Youth with a Mission* are among nationally known ministries that work with the Mission or provide items for distribution by the Mission these days; however, the primary support still comes from the participation of individuals and churches located throughout the United States.

Many of the Reservation churches served by the Mission are still in small buildings with no electricity, wood-stove heat, outhouse-type bathrooms—and people hungry for the Word of God. For example, recently at Teec Nos Pos, twenty-one people were baptized in a portable tank. Water to fill the tank had to be hauled four miles. One man hitchhiked nearly eighty miles to be baptized that morning.

Besides the activities mentioned above, the Cartwrights are also working on taping programming for local Christian TV and making teaching tapes that will multiply their efforts to help Reservation churches.

It is the desire of Many Waters Mission to promote awareness and prayer support for the churches on the Navajo Reservation. They recognize prayer as being a most important and beneficial way to support these churches—therefore Many Waters Mission has introduced an Adopt-a-Church program as one method of accomplishing this goal of sustained prayer support.

People who are interested in helping finance the work of the mission, participating on work teams, adopting a church, or volunteering their individual time and talents at Many Waters Mission will find more information on their website at *www.manywatersmission.org*.

You may contact the Mission at:
Many Waters Mission
#3 Road 6820
Waterflow, NM 87421.

Phone (505) 598-5433.
Fax (505) 598-0725.

On the Web at *www.manywatersmission.org*

Wheatfields community today

Wheatfields Church today

Lynn inside a Reservation church today

Many Waters Mission in Waterflow New Mexico today

CPSIA information can be obtained
at www.ICGtesting.com
Printed in the USA
BVHW030552060423
661863BV00001B/7

9 781600 342967